love

will steer me true

D0034085

Other Books by Jane Knuth

Thrift Store Saints

Thrift Store Graces

love
will steer me true

**A Mother and Daughter's Conversations
on Life, Love, and God**

JANE & ELLEN KNUTH

LOYOLAPRESS.
A JESUIT MINISTRY
Chicago

LOYOLAPRESS.
A JESUIT MINISTRY

3441 N. Ashland Avenue
Chicago, Illinois 60657
(800) 621-1008
www.loyolapress.com

Cover art credit: Kitigan/Shutterstock.com.

ISBN-13: 978-0-8294-4143-7
ISBN-10: 0-8294-4143-3
Library of Congress Control Number: 2014947065

Printed in the United States of America.

14 15 16 17 18 19 Bang 10 9 8 7 6 5 4 3 2 1

For my daughters, Ellen and Martha. Thank you for sharing your faith stories with me. You know I love that kind of stuff.

—Jane

For my family, who have been listening patiently to my daily chronicles for years.

—Ellen

Contents

Prologue   ix

1   The Other Side of the Planet   1

2   Two Hours by Bullet Train   5

3   Junko   9

4   God and His Clear Instructions   15

5   The Gift   19

6   Saved   25

7   Jizo   29

8   Worry and Prayer Aren't the Same Thing   35

9   Ayden   39

10   Ito Sensei Singing Out   47

11   Ambiguity   51

12   Guardian Angel and Jizo   55

13   Prayer and Parenting   61

14   Christmas   67

15   Rodger   71

16   I'll Call You in Your Morning   77

17   Commandments   79

18   Thrift Store Saints   85

19   Lambs and Dragons   87

20   In the Arms of a Faith Community   93

21 The Difference of One Vowel   97

22 Five-Fifteen A.M.   103

23 Coming Down   107

24 Folding Cranes   113

25 The Caring Network Luncheon   117

26 Over the Top of the World   123

27 The Sakura Are Late This Year   125

28 The Inside of the Pot   133

29 Lessons Learned   137

30 The Virgin Mary in My Zen Garden   141

31 Almost Ready to Go   145

32 "I Read Your Book Again"   149

33 Water Ranger   153

34 Ready to Listen   159

35 Feast of the Assumption Birthday   161

36 Weeds   167

37 Release   173

38 Prayer Beads   177

39 Caretakers of the Shrine   183

40 Meaning of the Jizo   187

Glossary   191

Acknowledgments   195

About the Authors   197

Prologue

Ellen

The sign warns of falling rocks, steep inclines, and snakes. Just in case any of us preparing for the climb can't read the complicated Japanese, our guide, a middle-aged monk clothed in robes and sandals, explains it with descriptive gestures.

A combination of circumstance, frantic life decision, and confused prayer has brought me to the foot of Mount Mitoku, a famous tourist destination in this region of Japan I now call home. An ancient temple perches so precariously on the side of the cliff face that legend says it was "thrown" there. This place is both a religious site and a great photo op, a must-see for any new arrival to Tottori Prefecture—a.k.a., me.

I like a hike now and then. I also like Japanese historical sites. I'm even rather fond of nature. I enjoy none of these things enough to contend with falling rocks, near vertical inclines, and snakes. However, feeling the need to prove my newly claimed title of "adult," I've once again jumped into a situation I'm not sure I'm ready for.

Now, as I step forward, courage barely in place, the Japanese monk blocks me. He frowns and shakes his head, gesturing at the ground.

"These are no good."

"What?" I peer down at my sneakers. "What's not good? My shoes?" I exchange a look with the young man behind me in line. "What does he mean?"

He shrugs. "Last year they had a few tourists fall off the trail and die, so the monks have the final say in footwear." We both look at the guide. "I think he wants you to change."

"But . . . I don't have any other shoes," I explain. "What can I—" Another monk trots forward and thrusts something into my hands. "Wait . . ."

My companion's eyebrows nearly disappear into his hairline. "Oh, *man*," he gasps, majorly amused. "Traditional grass sandals! Good luck climbing in those."

"I can't! Can I? No way!" But it appears I can and will, because before I can blink, my shoes are gone, the monk-approved sandals are on, and I'm being handed a pair of rough gloves meant to protect my hands from the chains we'll use to pull ourselves up the vertical parts of the mountain.

Deep breaths.

These sandals have surprisingly good grip, I tell myself, as I clamber up the first tree trunk step. *Maybe this won't be so bad?* The leaves rustle to my right, and I turn my head in time to see a snake disappear into the underbrush.

"Oh God."

Is it possible to pray and blaspheme at the same time?

1
The Other Side of the Planet
Ellen

It is only four days to my departure for my new adventure/job/life in Japan and yes, I am going shopping *again*. Despite a year of living in Japan during my study abroad program and being well aware what an efficient, abundant country it is, I have been obsessed with preparatory clothes shopping. My mother, a math teacher for many years, has been pointing out that perhaps I should be more concerned with preparing myself for the English teaching job I will be starting in less than a month. But, seriously, how can I focus on that when I haven't even found the flats I need to go with those pants I got last week?

My mom eyes the car keys dangling from my fingers and asks, "Have you had a chance to look over those teaching manuals yet?"

"I read through them already, Ma. Don't worry, I've got it." The keys in my hand remind me that I need to get the car interior vacuumed before I give it to my younger cousin. There's a gas station near the mall; I'll stop there on the way home.

My mom smiles at me. "I'm proud of you, Ellie. I can't believe how confident you've become. Will you be back for dinner?"

I nod and am out the door, but her kind words have roused the butterfly hordes that have camped out in my stomach since I got my acceptance e-mail two months ago. *Oh, if she only knew . . .*

I didn't lie; I have read the information pamphlets several times. I've researched the JET—the Japan Exchange and Teaching—program and looked up websites geared toward teaching English as a second language. I've cross-examined friends who've gone through the same placement program. I've even printed out all the available information about the small rural community where I'll be living—they grow pears, have a fishing port, and use a lot of energy wind turbines.

But the truth is, I have no idea how to teach English. I speak it rather well but have never taken a teaching class in my life. I'm a recently graduated international studies major, and though I've studied Japanese for several years, I am not a model student by any means.

Oh, and there's the issue that I'm going to be teaching at a junior high school.

Junior high. I don't remember my twelve- to fifteen-years-old period clearly because I've suppressed it. A panicky, sick feeling comes over me when I think back to the social roller coaster that was middle school. I also remember my classmates making our teacher cry from sheer frustration.

And now I'm going to be that teacher.

So I'm driving to the mall for the umpteenth time because even though I don't know how to teach, and I doubt I can cope with teenage angst, I do know how to shop. If I'm going to subject myself to the critical eyes of thirteen-year-olds every day, I may as well look stylish doing so, right?

Inside the mall I'm enveloped with a mix of blaring pop music, fluorescent lights, and the smell of pretzels. I make a mental note to stop by the pretzel shop before heading home. Despite the genius of Japanese cuisine, baking is not a national strength. Turning left at Hot

Topic, my destination appears in front of me: Forever 21. I'm about to turn twenty-four, so I guess I'm squarely in their target demographic.

The clerks smile when I walk in. I used to work at this mall, and several of them are my friends. They don't bother me as I dive into the racks. Mall employees extend a "no customer service" courtesy to one another. I'm glad because I really don't want to talk about my impending move.

I find the shoes I need. This is a relief because, at five foot seven with size nine feet, I am pushing the boundaries of Japanese sizes. Going from a medium to an extra-large in one plane ride is hard on a girl's ego. I also find a scarf I don't need, earrings that will probably be banned at my new workplace, and a skirt I'm not sure I'll ever wear, but it's sparkly. Walking to the register, I am distracted by a five-dollar rack.

I spot a simple, white tank top among the other discounted offerings. The word *Faith* is emblazoned across the front in big black letters. Leaning closer I can see the definition: "Trust, Confidence, Belief, Reliance."

I'm going to need a lot of faith. Not only in myself and the people around me, but also in the God I've been taught to love and trust since I was too small to reach the top of the holy water font. Japan is a **Buddhist/Shinto** nation, and though she hasn't said anything, I can tell my mother is worried about how my spiritual life is going to fare in a land so far removed from the cathedral-laden world I grew up in. I grab the shirt and add it to my pile. A tank top isn't something I can wear to work, but those words on the front will be a good reminder of what I need to maintain during the upcoming challenges.

And it'll look great with this sparkly skirt.

2
Two Hours by Bullet Train
Jane

Our daughter Ellen is neither frail nor shy, nor unpracticed in negotiating her way through airports. In her twenty-three years she has visited England, France, China, and Japan all by herself. Today, Dean and I and our younger daughter, Martha, are watching Ellen scan her passport through the check-in computer at Detroit Metro Airport. This time, her destination is Kotoura, Japan. Dean helps her heave the two bulging suitcases onto the scale, while Martha writes Ellen's name and address on the luggage tags. I am fingering my rosary in my coat pocket. There isn't much else for a mother to do at this point.

The airline clerk, a friendly young Asian woman, is chatty. "How long will you be travelling in Japan?" she asks Ellen.

"At least two years, I hope. I have a job teaching English."

"Two years? In Tokyo? I've visited there many times. You will enjoy it."

"No, not Tokyo. I'll be in the western part of the main island: Tottori Prefecture. Have you been there?"

"Tottori? Really? It is very remote. There are many mountains and . . . cows, I think."

"Cows?"

"Yes. Many cows." The clerk smiles determinedly. "The ice cream comes from Tottori. It is delicious. I am sure you will enjoy."

The check-in is complete and, freed from the heavy bags, we all move toward the open space in front of the security screening area. This is where we'll say farewell because only people with boarding passes may proceed further. Martha and I link our arms in Ellen's, and Dean checks the electronic departures board one last time. "It should leave on time," he tells her. "Your expected arrival is 5:00 p.m. tomorrow. That will give you plenty of time to catch your bus to the orientation. Did you change any dollars for yen?"

Ellen shakes her head. "I'll do it at Narita airport, before I catch the shuttle." I admire this child so much. She graduated from college only seven months ago. She is so confident. Where does this courage come from that makes her believe that international flights, cultural barriers, a different monetary system, and teaching children a new language, are within her abilities? How did she learn all this by her early twenties?

Ellen Marie was born on August 15, the Feast of the Assumption of the Blessed Virgin Mary into heaven. It is one of those feasts that non-Catholic Christians find suspicious because of its scarce biblical foundations. The feast is based on two thousand years of Catholic tradition passed from generation to generation. I am part of those generations, and I feel the obligation to pass on this truth. This is part of the issue between my generation and Ellen's.

My husband, Dean, a steadfast Lutheran, chose *Marie* as Ellen's middle name long before we knew which day she would appear. On my side of the family, both her Catholic grandmother and great aunt were beyond pleased with the choice of middle name, and told us so. I could tell from the bewildered look on his face that Dean was not even aware of the holy day. In the years following, Ellen was not overly happy about being obligated to attend Mass on her birthday, and I never was successful in helping her find the blessing in it.

Now I pull the rosary out of my pocket and hand it to Ellen. "I know you packed yours. Here, take this for the flight." This string of beads is what Catholics use to meditate on the events of Jesus' life through the eyes of his mother, Mary. It is a symbol of what I really want to give my daughter—except God isn't gift-able. God is not an object, nor is God an idea. God is a being. I can introduce these two to each other, but I can't start their conversation.

Did Dean and I teach our children to love God in order to keep them close to us? If so, then obviously, that isn't what's happening in this airport.

Or did we teach our children to love God in order to keep them close to him? If that's the case, then it shouldn't matter where they travel in the world. *You need to have a little faith, Jane.*

Ellen pockets the beads and doesn't argue. She is kindhearted.

"As soon as you can, find a church, okay?" I tell her.

"We talked about this, Ma. That's not going to be possible. The coordinator of the program told me that the nearest Christian church is two hours away by bullet train, remember?"

"Still, there must be some kind of church in your town."

"There are always Buddhist temples and Shinto shrines, lots of them. Don't worry. I'll be fine."

Two other families join us in the open space in front of the barriers. Ellen greets a young woman approximately her age whom we have met before. She is another eager Midwesterner who's seeking her future in the Far East. They both turn and wave happily to a young man who has one arm over the shoulders of his teary-eyed mother.

I know how that mother feels. I will not look at her or I may end up the same sniffling mess. I will send my daughter out the door with faith. She will have my rosary, not my tears.

Ellen's too-bright talkativeness warns me that she is already close to an emotional meltdown, and my tears won't help. I am determined not to cry. I pull out my camera instead and hide behind it. We meet the other families and take photos with one another's cameras. All the passing of cameras back and forth and the rearranging of groups takes up the remaining time. I don't know it now, but soon I will be very grateful for these photos.

This is the moment. We hug and whisper, "Love you" straighten collars, hug again, and they are gone. The other mothers, with fingers against their mouths, fumble for tissue as they turn away.

I am strong. I take Martha's arm, and Dean leads us to the escalator toward the parking ramp. I do not shed a tear until I step on the first moving step and let go of Martha's hand. "Don't even think about moving out of the country until Ellen comes back," I tell her.

Martha gapes at me in surprise. And then my tears fall.

3
Junko

Ellen

The whirlwind of arrival, first introductions, TV appearances, newspaper interviews, and parties is over. Or at least I hope so. I can't imagine that there is anything else about the new junior high English teacher that anyone can possibly be interested in. The local cable has even broadcast what my favorite color is (red), which is the reason I came home to a lovely bouquet of red carnations on my doorstep the other day.

Today is my first official day of work, and I've carefully chosen a collared shirt and suit skirt to wear. Since it's summer vacation, people will be dressed casually at the office, but I still want to make a good first impression. I've already met most of the teaching staff, and hampered as I am by communicating in my second language, I'm putting faith in the power of second, third, and fourth impressions to push things in my favor.

Thanks to jet lag, I'm still waking up hours before I need to, so I have plenty of time to eat breakfast, brush my teeth, check e-mail, and brush my teeth again. My plan is to leave my apartment at 7:45 and arrive at 7:50. School begins at 8:15. According to all the orientation pamphlets, I've read, on-time is late. Twenty-five minutes early should be enough of a cushion against cultural ignorance.

It's an unbearably hot day, but I've decided to walk the half mile to school anyway. I am now the owner of a teeny, tiny Japanese car, but I'm still terrified of driving on what my brain screams is the wrong side of the road. On top of that, four-foot-deep, open storm sewers run parallel with the sidewalks in my neighborhood and gurgle their way under each intersection. Because the houses hug the narrow streets, these intersections are blind corners optimistically equipped with concave mirrors and yield signs. There's no room for sudden swerves or tiny errors of judgment, so until I'm forced behind the wheel, it's leg power for me.

From my fifth-floor balcony, I've already mapped out the route and am confident I won't lose my way. I'm out the door exactly on time and begin walking to school. As I pass the train station, I see a group of people waiting for the bus, so I offer a falsely confident "Good morning" in my most polite Japanese. They stare at me without answering, but I just keep smiling. *They'll get used to me, surely.*

I climb the pedestrian bridge over the tracks, and at the top I take a minute to appreciate the view of the surrounding neighborhood with its little gardens and shiny tile roofs. I'm entranced by Japanese architecture. It's not as dramatic as the buildings in China or Malaysia, but to me, the charm of the unpainted gray siding, undulating tile, and sliding paper walls is unmatched. Down at street level again, I cross the first small road uneventfully. I can see the school now, a little more than two blocks away. At the second intersection, I stop. Which way to look first before crossing—right and then left? I think that's correct. I wait for a car to pass me and take a step out into the street.

I hear a sudden squeal of brakes, and brace to be flattened by a very compact car. *What a way to go—the press will have a field day.* But nothing happens. I crack my eye open; the road around me is empty. *Phew.* But then what . . .?

A car door slams, and I realize the screeching sounds were caused by the vehicle I let pass seconds before. The car is now purring calmly in the middle of the road. The driver has activated the hazard lights, and a small woman with a no-nonsense bobbed haircut jumps out of the car and runs straight for me.

What have I done now? Should I apologize for something? Surely I didn't break any unspoken cultural rules in the five-minute walk to school? Was I supposed to look left and then right?

"Hello, hello!" She runs up to me, unconcerned that her car is blocking one-half of the two-lane road. I can see two small heads through the back windows. "You are the new English teacher!"

"I . . . yes . . ." Is it okay to leave the car running with the kids in it? "Yes, hello. I'm Ellen."

"I am Junko. I see you on TV!" My hand is seized and shaken vigorously. "Kotoura is so happy. Welcome!"

It seems that, instead of admonishing me, she just wants to introduce herself. It's strange to be doing this in the middle of a street, but I can't help but smile. I give up on the idea of being early for school. "It's nice to meet you, Junko."

"I want you to come to my house," she declares. "My friends want to meet you, and we can eat cake. Are you free on Saturday?"

I'm sure they told me during orientation that being invited to visit someone's house is rare, but it seems that, as with everything else, Kotoura is determined to reverse my expectations. "Yes, I'm free Saturday."

"I will pick you up at 9:45 on Saturday morning," she tells me. "I know where you live."

Oh. Well then. I make a mental note that I should start thinking up some secrets about myself because I have none. Then we are shaking hands again and Junko is back in her car and driving away. I continue up the hill toward school and, peering carefully at the traffic mirrors (mirrors installed at blind corners), cross the final street without incident.

On Saturday morning Junko arrives at my apartment at exactly 9:45. I climb into her car, confronted by the two small children I glimpsed earlier. A four-year-old girl and her three-year-old brother are battling each other for some sort of action figure. Though I have no doubt it is meant to be a superhero, it doesn't look like he'll be saving anyone in his one-legged state.

"Ruka, let Isaiah have Kamen Rider!" Junko admonishes them in Japanese. "Say hello to Ellen **Sensei**." Ruka pays her mother no attention, but I'm instantly curious.

"Your son's name is Isaiah?" I ask her. "That's not a Japanese name, is it?"

"Ah, no, I'm sorry it isn't," she says. "My husband and I met when we were on a service mission in Tonga, so we wanted to give one of our children a Tongan name."

"You lived in Tonga?" I'm astonished. Of all the things I expected of this small-town housewife, a stint as a foreign aid worker in Tonga was not one of them. "What did you do there?"

"I was an abacus teacher." She's concentrating on backing her car down the narrow alleyway that leads to her house. "Do you know how to use an abacus?" I admit I don't, and she smiles as she parks the car successfully in her tiny front garden area. "The local community center gives classes to children every Sunday morning, I'm sure you could join."

We gather the kids from the backseat, take four steps across the gravel yard, and enter her cheery, friend-packed living room. Junko's two-story home is brand new; it's filled with hardwood floors, large open spaces, and a dozen toddlers and their mothers. The rest of the morning, I meet more people than I can remember and hold more babies and small children than I've ever held in an entire year. The mothers are thrilled when I talk to the babies in English. They're sure that even my wordless coos are prepping them for speaking foreign languages. I'm skeptical because these little ones don't even speak much Japanese yet, but the way these cute, black-haired babies stare at me and grab my nose makes me wonder if I'm the first foreigner they've encountered. It makes me more determined than ever to be not only a good teacher, but a good ambassador.

Later that evening I'm relaxing on the woven floor in my apartment when my cell phone rings. I hear Junko's cheerful voice. "Thank you so much for today! My friends were very happy to meet you." I respond in kind. The young mothers in the group were all lovely. "We want to meet you every month," Junko continues. "Is it okay to schedule the next **Ellen-kai** [Ellen meeting]?"

After a moment's consideration, I agree. Junko exclaims happily, and as she chatters on, I grab my scheduler to pencil in our next play-date. I have a feeling that this is the beginning of a long friendship.

4

God and His Clear Instructions

Jane

Lake Michigan is swirling around my ankles as my toes sink into the sand with each lap of the waves. Fifteen feet southwest of where I am standing, two seagulls hang-glide in the breeze. They watch my hands, pondering the edibility of my pen and notebook paper, but eventually decide to move downwind to where my six colleagues are grouped together in a lively discussion. On a beach that shouts summer vacation, two days before the beginning of the academic year, my fellow teachers and I are on a faculty retreat for our Catholic school.

I should join them.

At this moment we are supposed to be sharing our ideas about "**catechesis** in the classroom." I'm a math teacher, and I have zero ideas about how to teach religious principals in geometry class. Instead, I turn toward the horizon and share some ideas with God.

God, you know I've always taught math to community college students. What's up with this job you've dropped in my lap? Eighth graders? I have never been fond of eighth graders. When I was an eighth grader, I didn't even like myself. In my memory, junior high was a place where childhood dreams smothered and died.

But math teachers are hard to find, and I was offered the position as junior high geometry instructor because the school was desperate, because they know I am qualified, and because, from their point of view, I don't appear to be working right now.

I glance down at the notepad and pen in my hand. The waves are breaking two feet in front of me and splashing droplets onto the paper. I should be writing something down to share with the other teachers. But I don't want to write anything.

I know a little bit about writing—that's not the issue. In the past few years I have published a few magazine articles, written a regular column in the Catholic newspaper, and now harbor a deep feeling of purpose in completing a book manuscript about the volunteer work I've done for the **St. Vincent de Paul Society.** Dean has been ever so patient and encouraging while I shopped the manuscript to various publishers, a process that requires weeks, sometimes months, for each submission. While I have puttered around with improving my writing and adding stories, there has been a lengthy pause in employment as a teacher. Tutoring math is wedged in between writing and submitting the book to publishers and collecting a bounty of rejection letters. Meanwhile, not much money is coming in.

God, you seem to be speaking more clearly than usual. Rejection letters are difficult to misinterpret. A job offer, when I didn't even apply, is also hard to argue against. But seriously? Eighth graders?

Fourteen-year-old geometry students are at the top of their class academically. They aren't delinquents, and the class size won't be overly large; nothing to worry about there. My pupils will be well-prepared and bright.

From what I've been reading in the latest pedagogic manuals, this age group craves personal attention, rejects personal advice, thrives on social acceptance, and randomly excludes peers from groups. Clothing and personal hygiene—whether their own or everyone else's—have recently become central in their awareness. They cling to the unrealistic expectation that schoolwork can be mastered during class time, and they quickly lose interest in topics that are either below their level or too challenging. They'll do the homework, but are not overly concerned if their answers are correct. They assume that the answers in the book are wrong, not theirs.

I'm going to have to solve every single problem in that entire textbook before I assign them, and after thirteen years of teaching math, I am weary of solving math problems. The one bright spot is that Ellen is teaching students of the same age, and it will give us something to share in a relationship that doesn't seem to have much else in common.

And rejection letters are difficult to misinterpret. I stuff the pen in my pocket and wade toward shore. Maybe junior high is still the place where dreams smother and die.

5

The Gift

Ellen

The small fourth-grade girl standing in front of me stares up into my face for several seconds before determinedly sticking out her hand. With a smile, I clasp it in my own and gently shake it up and down. "It's nice to meet you."

"Yes." She nods once, releases my hand, and returns to her desk, bravery allotment for the day depleted. Her tablemates welcome her back, impressed by her mastery of this most Western of greeting techniques.

"Nice job!"

"Hahaha Shoko, you spoke English!"

"You're supposed to say 'thank you.' Not 'yes'!"

"Alright, settle down!" The homeroom teacher's voice cuts through the rising chatter. "Quiet! Congratulations, Shoko, on winning the rock-paper-scissors contest. Wasn't that a nice prize to shake the new English teacher's hand?" Several kids are visibly distressed that they missed out on the chance, and the teacher hurries to distract them. "Ellen Sensei will be here in Kotoura for a long time, so don't worry—you'll all get your chance."

A long time, huh? Though my current plan is to stay in my new town for at least two years, I'm not sure if that's what the teacher means. There is a small portion of the populace already hard at work to convince me to stay forever. Pretty certain that's not going to happen. I'll have to be sure to shake all their hands before I go.

It's my first day of teaching elementary school, and though I'm not sure what I expected, it wasn't this. Since I arrived at 8:30 this morning, I've given an awkward speech to the entire student body, repeated my planned self-introduction about six times, and faced off against thirty-five fourth graders in an ultimate rock-paper-scissors battle in which I'm not sure I understood the rules.

The children are adorable. The girls' shiny black hair is neatly styled, and the boys' sticks up in a variety of wild cowlicks. Dressed alike in school-issued navy blazers, their bright brown eyes follow my every move, so naturally I start to fidget. They are giggly, affable, and extremely interested in Ellen Sensei. I turn to find three of them carefully picking up a strand of hair that has just detached itself from my shirt sleeve and floated to the ground.

"Um . . . what are you doing with my hair?"

The boy who has the follicle draped over his pencil regards me seriously. "Your hair is *gold*. Is this natural? Do you dye it?"

"Actually, it's brown," I point out. "Yes, it's natural. See? My arm hair is the same color."

They all lean in close to see. "It's so soft!" a girl declares. "Like cat hair!"

I snatch the strand of hair off the pencil and shush their protest. "It is *my* hair," I assert. "I'm taking it back." The teacher motions me to the front, and I dutifully return.

Nodding once, the teacher informs the students of how the class will end. "We have fifteen minutes left, so we're going to have a 'question corner,' okay? You can ask Ellen Sensei any question you want."

A boy's hand shoots up. "Sensei, we can ask *any* question?"

The teacher waits until I nod. "Yes, anything."

It's as if a dam has broken, that's how quickly the inquiries come flowing out.

"What's your favorite color?"

"Do you like fermented soy beans?"

"How many sisters do you have?"

"How did you come to Kotoura?"

"Do you play baseball?"

Most of the answers are pretty straightforward, and I'm able to keep pace. A few catch me off guard: "What kind of house do you like?" "Have you ever shot a gun?" And there are the standard embarrassing ones: "How much do you weigh?" "Why is your Japanese accent wrong?" A slim boy in the front row raises his hand for the first time, and I choose him.

"Which **Naruto** character is your favorite?" he asks, eyes locked on my face.

Naruto is a popular comic book about ninjas that has spawned an equally popular animated TV show. The show is so successful it is syndicated in the United States. Luckily, eight years of working part-time in a bookstore has given me a solid grounding in this most important of Japanese literature. "I like the ninja teacher, *Kakashi*," I tell him. "*Shikamaru*, the really smart ninja, is cool, too." My student nods and sits back. Immediately, another hand is up in the back of the room.

"Yes?" This hand is also attached to a young boy, but at his shoulder, a teacher's aide is crouched, whispering intently in the child's ear.

The boy giggles and stands. "Do you have a boyfriend?"

I knew this was coming, it's just surprising it took them this long. It was the second question the JHS principal asked. "Nope. No boyfriend."

Instead of the usual surprised laughter, the boy has a declaration ready. "Sensei says he likes you!" The teacher's aide rises from his crouch and sends a jaunty wave my way. All the kids shriek in amusement, and I'm left alone to smile my way out of it.

The main teacher steps in, and we're back to the interview marathon.

"How old are you?"

"What does your dad do?"

"What does your mom do?"

"Who do you like better, your mom or your dad?"

I spear this questioner with a glance. "Wait a second, how can I answer that? Who do *you* like better?"

She grins at me. "I like my grandma best."

Tricky, tricky, tricky, these kids.

One "question corner" session is probably enough to turn anyone into a diplomat. I glance at the clock, so everyone glances at the clock, and it's clear we've exceeded the class time by five minutes. The teacher rushes us through closing salutations and reminds all the kids to "touch" (read: high-five) me on the way out.

The students are still asking questions as they leave the room. A few stop to recite some of the English words they know; some of them just want to give me a hug. The group of three who were denied their strand of hair each demands another to take home to show their parents. I refuse gently but firmly. It doesn't seem like a good precedent to set. The room starts to clear out, and when the last child reaches me, I recognize him as the boy who asked me about my favorite ninja.

"Hey, thanks for your question." I high-five him and smile at his serious little face. "So which character is your favorite?"

"I like Kakashi, too," he tells me and retrieves something from his back pocket. It's a tin pencil case, emblazoned with the *Naruto* show artwork. Colorful ninjas cartwheel across the surface, and "throwing stars" (ninja weapons) fly about haphazardly between posed confrontations. This is a well-loved possession, as evidenced by the dents and scratches across the shiny surface. He opens it to reveal a set of pencils, all in their own holders, each dedicated to one particular character.

"Oh, these are really cool!" Each pencil even comes with a cap. I'm impressed by his collection and tell him so, "You really love this show, don't you?"

He nods and pries the Kakashi-themed pencil out of its central placement. "Here." He thrusts it out toward me. "I'm giving you this."

"I . . . what?" Even in this pristine collection, it's obvious that this pencil has special standing. It's longer than the others, gently used. "No, you can't! Kakashi is your favorite character."

"He's your favorite character, too." The little boy places the pencil in my hand and shuts the case with a definitive snap. "So I want you to have it. You don't have one, do you?"

I shake my head, and for the first time he smiles. "Good. Thanks for class, Ellen Sensei. Come back again, okay?"

And he's gone.

I'm left standing alone in the classroom, mouth open, heart full. For a fourth-grade boy to gift his most precious possession to a foreign woman he's never met before, simply because they both liked the same thing—what level of kindness and selflessness does that require? And does he know how happy he just made me?

I ponder the pencil and finally pocket it as I walk back to the staff room. I'm going to keep this pencil, I decide, as a reminder of what kind of person I want to become. I want to be as kind as this fourth grader. I want to be as open to reaching out to strangers.

I want to be worthy of receiving such a selfless gift.

6

Saved

Ellen

Today is my day of rest. Not in the biblical sense, because it's Saturday, but in the I-have-nothing-scheduled-today-and-plan-to-eat-only-pop-corn sense. Today is sacred.

Which is why the sound of my doorbell ringing so disturbs my emotional peace. I frown at the closed steel portal, wracking my brain for why anyone would trek up five floors of stairs to interrupt my after-noon. I haven't ordered anything from Amazon, so it won't be the post-man. I haven't been playing loud music, so it won't be the neighbors. And I'm relatively sure I haven't broken international law this week, so chances are slim that the authorities are here to deport me.

The doorbell rings again. I sigh and go open it.

"Good afternoon. We're here to bring you the good news about Je—Oh!" I'm not sure which of us is more surprised: me, or the nicely dressed Mormon missionaries on my stoop. We stare at one another for a few seconds, and they recover first. "What a surprise! We didn't know you lived here."

By "you" I'm assuming they mean a foreigner, as opposed to me specifically. Everyone in this town knows I live here, so they must just be passing through. "Ha-ha, yes, I do. Surprise!" We all laugh a little nervously and look at one another again. I can read the pamphlets in their hands upside down. *Church of the Latter Day Saints* is printed across the cover. I had no idea there were Japanese Mormons, but here they are.

"Do you like Japan?" one asks me. "Isn't it lonely for you to live here?"

"I get homesick sometimes," I admit. "But everyone in Kotoura is wonderful; they take good care of me."

"And the food? Do you like the food?" I answer in the affirmative, and the questions keep coming quick and fast. Three minutes pass with me standing in the doorway and them eagerly questioning me about my impressions of Japanese culture, and I start to get a little worried. Am I supposed to bring up the purpose of their visit? Should I not mention it and maybe they'll forget? Finally the suspense gets to be too much for me and I nod to the reading material in their hands.

"These pamphlets, did you bring them for me?"

"Oh, yes!" They're a bit flustered but recover and thrust the bilingual brochures toward me. "Have you been saved?"

"I'm doing okay." I accept the papers and notice that they're almost exactly like the ones we get at home in the United States. Same softly sketched Jesus, same sunset in the background, same blond-haired angel. I momentarily wonder if any money could be made in an ethnic angel series and then chastise myself for getting off track. "Thank you, but I already believe in Jesus."

They blink at me, and I catch my mistake, switching to the Portuguese pronunciation. "Sorry, Jesús and Maria. I know all about them. I was raised a Christian."

Christianity was originally introduced to Japan by Portuguese priests, and to this day, translations of biblical names have a distinctly Portuguese pronunciation. It's fascinating from a historical point of view and cringe-worthy considering how badly the early foreign missionaries fumbled in their dealings with the shogun warlords.

"Yes, we see. But do you believe in Jesus?" they press, and I try to restate my point.

"Yes, I do. I know all about him. Maybe not the same way you do, but I learned about him in school. I believe in God."

"Hmm, yes, but have you really been saved?"

This is a hard question, because I honestly won't know the answer until it's too late to do anything about it. What's remarkable is how similar this conversation is to the ones I've had with these missionaries' brethren in America. It seems that, regardless of language, the same misunderstandings always arise. I decide to approach this from the tried-and-true method.

"Yes. You see, I went to Catholic school."

They stop. "So sorry?"

"Catholic." I tap my chest. "My mother is Catholic, I believe in Jesús and Maria. I pray the rosary."

"Oh." One of them thrusts the pamphlets into my hands and bows. "We understand. But please read these, they may help you."

"Yes, thank you." They're both nice people, and I have no hard feelings, just no need for saving. We all bow to one another, and they tell me they'll stop by next time they're in town. I smile and back into my apartment entryway, locking the door between us. *Phew.* I leave the brochures on my table, not sure if I'll read them later or not. My do-nothing afternoon beckons, and I retreat back to my living room.

Half an hour later, my doorbell rings again. "Seriously?" I mutter. "No way." I take sneaky steps to my peephole, which reveals two different, equally nicely dressed gentlemen standing on the other side of the door. "Oh man." Steeling myself, I swing the door open, girded for battle.

"Good afternoon! We're here to bring you the good news about—" they begin cheerfully, but I hold up my hand to stop them.

"No, no thank you. It's okay, I don't need it." They stare at me in confusion. "I'm a Christian you see, a Catholic, I'm fine. I don't need it." They look at each other, and I seal the deal. "The pope in Italy? Great guy, love him."

"Ah. Is that so?" They shift their feet and shuffle their papers. Finally one bows to me and hands me a pamphlet. "We understand. But if you ever change your mind and would like to change your cable TV package, please don't hesitate to call us." They bow their way down the hall, leaving me open-mouthed and holding information about a service-expansion offer.

Well, damn.

7

Jizo

Ellen

It's another Saturday morning, but this time I'm at school. Not because I have to be, but because everyone else is here and I'm feeling left out. The only things that Japanese students pursue with more intensity than their studies are their club activities. They practice their chosen sport or discipline six days a week, for up to four hours a day. Every Saturday morning, hours before I've changed out of my pajamas, I have watched, astonished, as kids biked past my apartment building headed to practice. I've listened with equal perplexity as teachers (all of whom double as a coach for one of the teams) grumble about weekend trips to other prefectures for regional championships or national qualifiers.

When do any of them get a chance to spend time with their families? This schedule seems intense for junior high school, but then again, most of the school culture here is intense.

I've gone to watch the after-school practices a few times and have found the students to be more relaxed and talkative than during class. It occurred to me that to be accepted not only as an okay person in the teens' eyes, but as a legitimate member of the teaching staff, I'm going to have to donate some of my Saturday mornings to the cause. So here

I am, barely awake, ready to figure out this aspect of Tohaku Junior High School.

Merely watching the practices doesn't sit quite right with me, though. For one, I'll be bored. For another, I'm worried they'll ask me to join in. I'm a competent athlete, but one look at these practices, and I know it can only end in tears for both my muscles and my dignity.

So I'm going to clean the school grounds.

I was raised in a family oriented toward volunteering. Every weekend of my young life involved some sort of charitable work. Soup kitchens, thrift shops, toy drives, blood drives, charity walks, clothing collections—you name it, I've done it. Granted, this mostly involved trying on donated clothing and sharing cash-register duties at the thrift store with my sister. If there's anything I learned from hours of pairing socks and counting the pieces of pre-owned puzzles, it's that there is always something in this world that needs cleaning or fixing. All you need to do is find it.

In this case I'll be picking up debris from the practice grounds that surround the school. While searching with the students for a lost tennis ball the week before, I noticed a number of abandoned umbrellas and discarded coffee cans in the bushes. It won't necessarily be fun, but it'll give me an excuse to be around while the kids practice. And maybe picking up trash now will atone for all the times I've thrown away my plastic bottles instead of recycling them in accordance to the trash pick-up sheet posted in my apartment.

I grab a pair of work gloves and a trash bag from the teachers' room, head outside, and begin collecting the trash. Kids running past me on their umpteenth lap of the track yell cheerful "hellos," and the baseball players remove their caps and thank me politely as I toss back errant baseballs. I've worked my way around half the field to the back corner by the pool entrance when I see it.

I first notice the strange way the tree is growing. Though the upper branches have straightened themselves out in their reach for the sunlight, the lower trunk is slightly bent. As I come closer, I can see that it has partially grown around, and partially dislodged, one of three low, connected cement walls. Setting down my trash bag, I brush aside the leaves and branches. Before me is revealed a small statue, no larger than a bag of rice. I feel a faint thrill as the Asian history geek in me recognizes what I've found.

It's a **jizo***!*

In the Buddhist tradition, **Ojizo-sama** is arguably the most well-known and most frequently seen Japanese divinity. From my studies, I know that jizos are supposed to guard children, so it makes sense that there would be one here on the school grounds where hundreds of children spend most of their week. Unfortunately, this particular jizo seems to have been forgotten.

The jizos I've seen before—and they are everywhere in Japan—have often been dressed in bright red bibs and surrounded by offerings of coins and sake. On inspection, this jizo, too, has received offerings in the past. I can see a lot of coins, although they are clumped together by dirt and weeds. Abandoned flower sconces full of water and muddy leaves have tipped behind the tree. I dig out a chipped sake cup that has fallen to the side of the statue. Past the crud, I can see some carefully written mantras. Amid the calls of the students practicing behind me, I'm struck by an idea.

I'll adopt this jizo, clean him up, and get him back into child-protection mode. I'm not sure I believe he actually works, but it can't hurt, can it? It's the same as hedging your bets by wearing a **Miraculous Medal**. *And*, I think as a baseball clangs off the fence, *these teens can use all the protection they can get.*

Seized with new energy, I pick up the little cup and hurry back to the school office. The school secretaries, three long-suffering women, look up as I rush in. "Good morning, Ellen Sensei."

"Do you have a hand saw?" I inquire. Seeing their wary looks, I hasten to explain, "You see, I found this little statue under a tree, and I want to clean him up and clear some of the branches."

The oldest of the three takes in a breath. "Ah, the Ojizo-sama! I forgot there was one. He's been there awhile, hasn't he?"

I shrug. "I'm not sure, but I want to clean him up."

She smiles. "You're a challenger, Ellen, but you can't cut the branches. That will anger the Shinto gods of the tree."

This makes me pause. "But . . . isn't the jizo statue a *Buddhist* tradition?"

She's nodding as she grabs a brush from the cupboard. "Well, yes, but you can't upset the Shinto tree god just to clean the Buddhist statue." She spots the sake cup I'm clutching. "Oh, you've found the offering cup."

"Yes, but I'm not sure what to put in it."

The three of them share a conferring glance. "Normally it's sake, but we can't have alcohol on school grounds. Why not use water? Here, you can wash it in the sink."

We clean up the cup and make a quick trip to the neighboring grocery store for flowers. A few rapid tutorials on proper jizo cleaning, and I'm back out on the grounds, carefully brushing dirt off the statue's face and resisting an urge to pull the weeds surrounding it; I don't want to anger the weed gods either. After half an hour of hard work, he looks much better. Surrounded by bright purple flowers, with a fresh offering of water, he's ready to protect the students as they finish practice and head out to enjoy their weekend.

Dragging the trash bag to the collection point, I make a little promise to myself to take care of Ojizo-sama. I might not understand everything he's about, but I do understand shrines. It'll be a good excuse for me to continue my school-ground pilgrimages—moments each day to be alone and sort through problems and questions.

8

Worry and Prayer Aren't the Same Thing

Jane

Why am I here?

Where am I going?

Whether we find ourselves sleeping on the street or sleeping in a palace, everyone asks these questions. Whether we are twenty-three years old or fifty-one, the uneasy sense of being disoriented travelers hangs over our heads.

Both Ellen and I are seeking answers, but we are not asking each other. At this moment, a world apart, the parent-child relationship is no longer the sweet sharing of victories, losses, and endless questions. The questions have stopped somewhere in the middle of my valuable advice, my thoroughly reasoned apologetics, and my avalanche of nagging. I have spent decades glimpsing Jesus in the writings of saints, in the mystery of forgiveness, in the ancient dialogue of liturgy, and in people who are suffering. This sheep-herding carpenter shows up when I need his strength, and waits patiently by when I muddle around with my unhelpful schemes for making myself and everyone else perfect. Ellen doesn't read the books I give her, she doesn't attend Mass or go to confession. She is still the loving, giving person who will bend over backwards to cheer a person who is glum, who will make each new acquaintance into a friend, and who never clings to a grudge. She talks to Jesus, she acts like Jesus, but she doesn't often want to come to his house. Jesus seems to be telling me not to worry about that too much, but I ignore his advice because he never worries enough for my taste.

There are no more chances to brace Ellen for a universe created of troubles and difficulties. I can no longer warn her against the creeping disaster of a hardened heart. She refuses to hear me telling her to guard against too much wanting and getting.

Dean and I are left watching from a distance as she pulls away from us and—our biggest worry—away from God. What we don't yet realize is that Ellen isn't the only one in the family on a wayside spiritual journey.

We are cruising down I-94, halfway to the Detroit Metro Airport, with Martha who is going to visit her sister. Dean and I aren't able to take time off from work now, but we are planning to visit Kotoura later, perhaps during the springtime cherry blossom festival. From the driver's seat, Dean is teasing Martha about whether she packed enough clothing in her two bulging suitcases. Half the clothing is for Ellen, and most of it is shoes. Size nine is impossible to find in Kotoura. The conversation leaves me out because there is no place in it for my worries. To purposely cause my children to worry would be anathema to my last twenty-four years of mothering. I can't put my anxieties in Martha's suitcase, and I can't share them with the family. They lie on my lap in my clenched hands.

Dean glances at me. He knows that one of my biggest worries is about Ellen's religious isolation. Christians make up 1 percent of the population in Japan, and Kotoura has no Christian churches at all. Zero. He says to me, "I think Mary is just around the next curve, maybe we should say a little prayer together."

"Who?" I ask.

"You know, one of those homemade Mary-in-the-bathtub shrines. It's near exit 133, just west of Jackson."

"Seriously?"

"Haven't you ever noticed it?" He is genuinely surprised. He assumes I have internal radar for any kind of Catholic shrine.

Sure enough, after a couple of miles, we see a symmetrical hill on the north side of the highway, and at its rounded summit stands Our Lady of Grace in a blue-painted cast-iron grotto. Her hands are spread gently at her sides in a wistful blessing over her rushing children who are speeding past one hundred feet below. Dean begins the prayer, "Hail Mary, full of grace . . . " and I chant along with him in the moment we pass underneath. My jaw unclenches a little. It comforts me to pray this very Catholic prayer with my very Lutheran husband.

"How long has she been there?" I ask when we finish.

He shrugs. "No idea. The first time I noticed her was about ten years ago."

"Do you remember when I told you," I begin slowly, "how Ellen has been restoring that Buddhist shrine on the school grounds?"

"Uh huh."

"What do you think is going on with that?"

"I think she grew up with St. Francis in the backyard."

I glance sharply at him. "But St. Francis and Buddha are not the same thing."

"Shrines are a place to pray. Didn't we just finish praying under a Mary-in-the-bathtub shrine? It doesn't seem that different to me."

"Sure it's different: Mary and Francis are Christian, and Buddha is . . . *Buddhist.* Plus, the trees around the jizo have some kind of Shinto spirits attached to them."

He nods. "You know what? You're right. We need to create some balance on our side of the planet. One Francis is not enough to counter a jizo and several Shinto tree spirits. I've been thinking that it's long past time for me to nail some theses to the front door—that should help."

Martha thinks this is pretty funny.

Dean grins at me sympathetically. "Don't worry, Jane. *Pray*. Worry and prayer aren't the same thing."

"Okay, I'm trying. Anyway, I don't like the way worry makes me feel." For the next few miles, while Hail Marys chant through my head, I ponder the differences between worry and prayer. One thing I know for sure: I like the way prayer makes me feel. I like it a lot.

"I'm going to send Ellen a new Miraculous Medal. She gave hers to a friend who was having a stressful time adjusting." I look at Dean sideways. "Is that too pushy?"

He shakes his head. "She told you she gave hers away? That sounds to me like a hint for a new one."

I nod. "I'll send two—just in case she wants to give another one away."

In the seat behind me, Martha sighs.

9

Ayden

Ellen

Ayden is one of my nearest foreign neighbors in Tottori and my closest friend. After an initial introduction at a party, followed by a raucous all-night karaoke session during which we discovered our mutual love of cheesy pop songs, we are best friends.

Ayden is only a year older than I am, but he's already into his third year in the English teaching program. An athletic, energetic New Zealander, his reputation precedes him everywhere he goes. Teachers, students, locals—all have seen or heard of him, whether through his work, newspaper articles, or frequent TV appearances. One particular cooking show he hosted seems to haunt him. "It's a good thing the viewers couldn't taste what we made," he confesses with a wry smile. "It's even better they didn't understand all the swears we used when it started burning."

He is irreverent about most things and curious about everything. No matter the topic, he devotes his whole attention to it, asking a myriad of questions that by the end of the conversation it seems he knows more about the subject than the person who introduced it. I learn to weigh my words carefully, if only to be sure I can defend my position should it turn into a friendly debate.

I pour out my worries and questions to him, and he answers from his experience, reassuring me that I will someday understand the workplace rules and that my coworkers are probably not as frustrated with me as I think they are.

Hearing him speak Japanese is a revelation. He is one of the few people I've met who can communicate without clunky translated sentences. Instead he moves fluidly through the language, within its rhythm.

We're at a local festival together when we bump into one of his young students, who clutches a cute dog to her chest. "Ayden teacher! Hello!"

"Hey there, Yukiko. How are you?" He nods politely as her mother walks up behind her. "Good evening, Ms. Isoue."

The mother scrutinizes me. "Is she your girlfriend?" She asks him. No "hello," no checking to see if I, too, can understand her.

Ayden shrugs. "Maybe. She's pretty isn't she?" We've already been asked this question three times this evening, and he's given a different response every time. Though we are in no way romantically involved, he likes to give open-ended answers. "It adds to the mystery," he explains in English when I protest. "They like guessing more than actually knowing." Now he turns back to the little girl. "What's your dog's name?"

"Koro," she proclaims brightly, offering the dog to be petted.

"He's very cute," Ayden says, now switching to slow English so she can catch his meaning.

Yukiko shakes her head. "*She*, Ayden teacher, *she*."

He apologizes for his mistake, and they walk away. When they're out of earshot, he smiles triumphantly. "Did you hear that? She corrected my English pronoun. Only a fifth grader, but she's already got the difference between 'he' and 'she' like it's nothing. Amazing kid, hey?"

I don't say anything as we wind our way back to the car, but I feel that the more amazing of the two is probably Ayden. I listened to the same conversation and it never once occurred to me to marvel at the student's abilities. It's another example of what makes him such a good teacher. No matter when or where, he listens. I'm much better at talking.

As we buckle up and begin the drive back toward my place, I reflect a bit on our friendship. In only a few months, we've become close. However, I realize that this might not be what he thinks. For my part, I've unburdened all my thoughts and worries on him, and he has patiently soothed me. But in return, what have I given him? Not much probably. We roll down the windows of his tiny car and pull onto the highway as he fiddles with the radio.

I know he has relatives back in New Zealand: an older brother, mother, and father. Like me, he contacts his family by Skype two or three times a month. He came to Tottori right out of school, and though teaching English was never his dream, he has become one of the most respected **ALTs** (assistant language teacher) in the prefecture. He is professional and self-effacing, qualities highly prized in the Japanese workplace.

Now he plugs his iPod into the car's sound system and selects a song. "Give this a listen. She's a singer in New Zealand. I think you'll like her."

A beautiful, melodic voice fills the car as we cruise west toward the setting sun. I'm struck first by the quality of the singer's tone and then immediately drawn to the lyrics; they seem to be speaking exactly to where I am right now.

"*I am changing, less and less asleep. Made of different stuff than when I began.*"

"Wow, what a voice," I say. Ayden nods, and I turn up the volume to hear her better. The song swings into the chorus, and suddenly I'm presented with a lyric that is both beautiful and uncomfortable.

"You make all things new. When the world is falling down around me, I'll be found in you, still standing."

"Good words, hey?" Ayden takes his eyes off the road for a moment and looks at me. "What do you think of it?"

This is obviously a Christian song. And though I love it, I'm not sure how I feel about hearing it first in my present company. Ayden, for all his open-mindedness, is rather antiorganization. He embraces many points of view but dislikes those who follow any path of thought he finds closed and out of touch. Accordingly, I have never broached the topic of anything spiritual with him. I know he's an agnostic, and though it doesn't bother me in the slightest, I am afraid of owning up to my Christian upbringing.

Raised with a Catholic mother and a Lutheran father, I have had more than my share of catechesis and apologetics. Though my Lutheran baptism was ruled legit by the Catholic school I went to, I still made my First Communion twice to satisfy both churches. My parents, fully committed to their ecumenical marriage and to each other, offered nothing but love and support to my sister and me, but the same couldn't be said for others.

When I was eight years old, the parish priest took me and a little Russian Orthodox girl in my class down to the church and read us the Apostles' Creed, stopping to make sure we agreed with each line. When I asked why only the two of us had to do this, he replied that since my father didn't believe in this creed he wouldn't be automatically going to heaven. Though he hastened to reassure me that the same wouldn't be true for me, I was deeply shaken.

That night, in bed and in tears, I asked my dad why he didn't convert to Catholicism in order to go to heaven with the rest of the family.

Hugging me close, my dad said the words on which I would ultimately base my own spiritual journey:

"Well, Ellie, first of all, we say that very same creed in the Lutheran Church. But it's true I don't believe quite the same thing as that priest or even Mama. I do believe in the same God, and he lives in the same heaven. And there are lots of different roads that go there."

As an adult I've tried hard to open my mind and heart to other peoples' roads. I, too, have come to believe that there are many ways to the same heaven, but sometimes, in taking a tour of other peoples' routes, I've hit roadblocks. These are erected quickly and unexpectedly and usually after the person in question learns I come from a Catholic or Christian background. At the slightest mention of either, the doors close and the person retreats from the conversation, sensing an impending lecture or conversion attempt. Nothing could be further from my intentions, but I understand the reaction. Christians don't have a great track record for living peaceably among other beliefs.

"When time and space are through, I'll be found in you . . ."

Now this song has opened up my theological Pandora's box, and I'm not sure how to close it. On the one hand, I would like to change the subject as quickly as possible. On the other, it is so rare that Ayden presents the topic for discussion, I feel I can do nothing but reply to it.

I give a silent gasp of prayer. *God, give me grace.* Hesitantly, I say, "It kind of reminds me of my parents."

I sense his gaze. "Really? How so?"

"Hmm, because even when I'm feeling really lost or confused, I can always call home. And they know who I am, they've always known me. So even when I'm not sure what's right or wrong, they remind me of who I am and where my base is."

It's a shaky explanation at best, but there's actually a lot of truth in it. Though my parents might not be fully acquainted with adult,

Japan-living Ellen, they have a better idea than anyone of how I was raised and what's in my heart.

Well, anyone apart from God that is.

Ayden takes a moment to ponder my words and nods. "I can see where you're coming from. I guess I hadn't ever thought of the song that way before."

I sigh and relax a bit. Conversation trap avoided.

He raises an eyebrow at me. "You do know the song's about Him, though. Right?"

Ah. Caught.

"Well . . . yeah, it's pretty obvious." I admit, feeling both nervous and ashamed. "But I know you don't really believe in that stuff so I didn't want to, you know, bring it up."

"Yeah, but you didn't. I did." Ayden shrugs. "I figured you're a Christian from those medals you wear sometimes. You act like it, too."

"Oh?" I am honestly not sure if this is a good or a bad thing, sad as that is to admit. "Please don't get the wrong idea; I totally support other beliefs. I'm not anti-other religions or anything."

"I didn't think you were." He stops at a red light and regards me frankly. "Why is that?"

I can't answer right away because no one's asked me that before. Finally, I repeat to him almost verbatim the words my dad said to a tearful eight-year-old so many years ago.

Ayden takes a moment to think about this as I sweat it out in the passenger seat. I've never really shared this with anyone, and I'm afraid of how I'll feel if he rejects it. I've had people tell me their complaints about the Catholic Church or Christianity as a whole, but this is more personal. It'll really hurt if he disapproves.

I wonder if I can have my faith and my friendships too.

As it happens, he gives a long, slow nod and taps the steering wheel thoughtfully. "I like that. Your dad's a smart man."

"Yeah, he is."

We're pulling up to my apartment building, and Ayden stops the car. "Thanks for hanging out, the festival was fun." I reply in kind, but he's not done. "And thanks for the chat. I've been meaning to ask you about that stuff for a while."

This is surprising. "You have? Why?"

He smiles as he shifts the car into drive. "I thought you probably had thoughts about spirituality. Anyway, I'll give you a copy of this CD next time, okay?" He waves goodbye and is gone.

As I watch his car turn the corner, the lyrics echo in my head.

I'll be found in you.

10

Ito Sensei Singing Out

Ellen

In addition to his usual basket of teaching supplies, grammar posters, and grading books, Ito Sensei is carrying a boom box. This is new, and I'm intrigued. "Are we going to listen to music?" I ask.

"Yes, Ellen Sensei. Today, I will ask the students to sing." Rays hit his spectacles as we walk past a window, and I'm momentarily blinded. "I may not have told you, but I often teach through music."

"That's great." In a family full of musicians, I have the distinction of being labeled "most likely to break into song." Ito Sensei, a quiet, thoughtful English teacher, doesn't strike me as a music lover. I have been hesitant to suggest songs to use in class, not sure what the students will like. "I'm always singing at home," I add.

"Oh, really?" The corners of his mouth crease into a smile. "Then please sing with the students today. They would like to hear you." His British accent always increases when he is pleased, prompting a smile of my own.

"What song are we going to use?" I inquire, sliding the classroom door open for him.

"I think you may know it," he says. "It is called 'We Are the World'."

It takes me a moment. "The . . . Michael Jackson song?"

One of the students has heard me. "Michael Jackson! We very much love Michael Jackson!" A group of nodding students instantly forms. "Do you like Michael?"

I stare at their eager faces. "I . . . um . . . you *all* know Michael Jackson?"

"Yes! So cool!" A boy is pushed to the front of the group. "Yusaku can moonwalk. Yusaku, show her."

Sure enough, he can. But before I can ask why a group of rural Japanese middle schoolers are such fans of a recently deceased American pop star, the class starts, and Ito Sensei and I slip into team-teaching mode.

At the junior high level, classes are always team taught. The Japanese teacher (Ito) is the leader, planning the lessons and handing out final grades. The ALT (me) is brought in to assist with speaking and listening. Due to the number of classes and the size of the school, I visit each class only once a week. I teach with four different Japanese teachers, and each of them has his or her own teaching style and a different way of using me in class. With minimum time to prep for weekly classes, this style of teaching hinges on trust and improvisation.

Ito Sensei is the easiest for me to work with. One of the senior teachers at the school, he commands respect from staff and students alike. He has taught for thirty-plus years and is confident in his craft but humble in his approach. Having lived abroad, he is acutely aware of the struggles faced by a foreign employee and goes out of his way to address me politely, with the same respect he'd give a tenured professor.

I'm intensely grateful and reciprocate by doing my best not to mess up his lesson plans.

But now it turns out he likes Michael Jackson. It's not that I don't like Michael Jackson, but his heyday was well before my time. I know he's the King of Pop, but my initial memories are of the scandal and decline that haunted his last years. To find a group of young people genuinely excited about his music is a shock. Michael Jackson isn't really cool anymore, is he? His classic songs maybe, but this charity song? Will my image survive this?

Ito Sensei turns to me as he introduces the song to the class.

"Ellen Sensei also knows this song. Right, Ellen Sensei?"

"Yeah, but I've never sung it before."

"Really?" Ito Sensei's eyebrows rise. "But it is very famous."

"Oh yes, of course," I agree, trying not to appear hopelessly unaware of my own culture. "But it's . . . a little old."

Ito Sensei checks the back of the CD. "Ah, it was released in 1985." I can see the kids doing the math in their heads. How in the world we are going to convince a bunch of teenagers to sing this out loud in front of their peers, I have no idea.

"So was I," I point out, and the faster students catch my meaning.

"Same birthday!" they exclaim, and widen their eyes. "Wow, Ellen Sensei! So young!"

Despite my misgivings, in five minutes we're all humming along. The kids crack up as the more talented jokesters try to imitate Cyndi Lauper and Bruce Springsteen. But it's not all mocking; many furtively mouth the words, writing pronunciation notes in the margins. Ito Sensei nods at me, and I give up my preconceptions of '80s music and sing loudly, correcting the students as I move around the room.

I had been terrified of being judged, but in reality, the students love it when I sing loudly. I gain extra points for mimicking Kenny Rogers. There is something about this shared silliness that takes away the ever-present stress of junior high. The kids are eating it up. When they demand to sing the song a fourth time, it hits me: Ito Sensei has tricked us into learning.

I turn to look at him, but he's bent over a student's desk patiently explaining that we are the *world*, not the *word*. I hit the replay button on the boom box.

As we head back to the teacher's room after class, I thank him for the class and ask, "How did you know the kids would like that? I never would have guessed. And how did you know they would sing with you?"

He looks at me in surprise. "I didn't. I like that song, so I used it, but as you said, perhaps it is a bit old now." Ito Sensei smiles again. "They sang because they wanted to sing with you. That is thanks to your power, Ellen Sensei."

I recognize in this comment the skilled Japanese art of deflecting praise. But I also hear something else. I hear that he trusted me to sing the song he chose, and that thought warms me to my toes. "It's a good song," I admit. "Shall we sing another next week?"

"Yes, I think so," he agrees. "Do you know the band Chicago?"

Oh, boy. Better brush up on my oldies.

11

Ambiguity

Jane

We like someone because. We love someone although.
—Henri de Montherlant

Math is unambiguous, but my students are not.

On any given day, my ten eighth-grade geometry students can be bright and lazy, interested and dismissive, and simultaneously self-absorbed and self-unaware. They do not want to look at me directly, and they squirm if my eyes focus for any length of time on them. They prefer to talk to me with their gaze on a computer screen.

One student, Kathryn, wrote "I hate math" on her paper the first day of class. This same young woman comes to school every morning with all her homework complete and is the best at solving the toughest problems.

Kathryn particularly enjoys the logic puzzles I put on the board every morning about a fictional island whose population consists of exactly two types of people: knights and knaves. Knights are always truthful, and knaves always lie.

Today's puzzle reads as follows:

You are walking on the **Island of Knights and Knaves** when you come across two inhabitants, A and B.

You ask A, "Are you a knight or a knave?"

A answers, but you don't hear what he says, so you ask B, "What did A say?"

B says, "A said he is a knave."

The question: Is B a knight or knave?

My students love/hate these knights and knaves with a passion. They walk in the room, and the first thing they do is read the problem off the board. If the solution seems obvious, they shout it out. Of course for credit, they must walk through their logic, step by step, explaining their answer to the class.

The young woman who loves the knights and knaves and hates math is also shy and ultrasensitive to perceived criticism. Today she waits until all the others have made a crack at figuring out if B is a knight or knave, and failed. When I turn to her, Kathryn wants to explain the answer from her seat, but I ask her to stand at the white-board. Reluctantly, she moves to the front of the room and picks up the erasable marker. Her voice is low, and she doesn't make eye contact with anyone.

Her logic, however, is flawless.

"Well, I thought about A first. If you ask anyone on the island what they are, they will all answer: 'I'm a knight.' So A must have said that. Whether A was a knight or knave—it doesn't matter. That means B was lying. So B must be a knave." She glances at me for approval, and I am grinning.

All five boys howl in protest. "Why will *everyone* say they're knights?! How can you know that?" Before she can answer, one of the boys, Evan, says, "Wait, wait, WAIT! She's right. They will all say they're knights . . . so B is a knave." He explains it again to his friends, and eventually they frown, shrug, concede, and look at their female classmate with new respect. She is blushing but smiling happily as she takes her seat.

The tallest boy, Dan, who is president of the student council, says to me, "Okay. Give us another one."

"Tomorrow. One per day—I don't want to spoil you. Let's see your homework." They roll their eyes and get out their books.

"Hey, Mrs. Knuth," Hannah says. "Mrs. Matyas told us that your daughter lives in Japan."

"Yes, that's right," I answer. "Turn to page thirty-three."

In atypical unanimity, the other students look at me at once.

"Cool. Have you been there?"

"Yes, we visited her when she studied in Japan as a college student. Danny, put your answer to number five on the board, and Evan, number seven."

The next question is not one I expect. "Do you speak Japanese?"

"Sierra, number nine, please, and Kristen, eleven. No, I don't speak Japanese, but I learned the basic phrases you need to know to get by." No one is moving very fast to get those exercises on the board. Instead, their glances back and forth show that they are reevaluating their teacher.

"Say something in Japanese."

"Yeah! How do you say 'soccer'?"

"No—say 'computer.'"

I tap the textbook in front of me and point at the board.

"Please, please, please, Mrs. Knuth."

Book in hand, Dan walks to the board, and shakes his head at his friends. "Don't you guys know yet that you can't get Mrs. Knuth off the subject?"

Really? I didn't know I had that reputation. For some reason, this pleases me.

The rest of the students push themselves up from their desks and follow Dan to the front of the room. The geometry begins to develop in fits and starts, but they are doing it willingly enough.

"Tell you what," I say. "I will teach you one thing in Japanese every week. By the end of the year, you will have about forty words or phrases."

"Yes!"

"What's our first word?"

"Teach us something now."

I bow from the waist. "Arigato gozaimasu," I say solemnly, and I straighten up, walk to the board, and write it.

They repeat it eagerly, and I correct their pronunciation.

"Tell us what it means, Mrs. Knuth," says Matt.

"It's the most important thing you need to know," I answer, "in any language."

"Where's the bathroom?"

"How much does this cost?"

"I'm an American?"

"Nooo . . ." I answer, suppressing my smile. "It means 'thank you very much.' Now, finish those math problems on the board."

I am having a blast with these kids. Who would have guessed?

12

Guardian Angel and Jizo

Ellen

It's a sunny Tuesday, and we are about to head into a roaring storm. Due to the wave of noise coming from classroom 1-4, Ito Sensei and I have paused in the hallway outside. Ito Sensei, unperturbed, nods to me as I hesitate in front of the door. "Let's do our best," he says. "They'll get used to my teaching style eventually."

I paste a smile on my face as we walk in and take our places at the front. Ito Sensei begins to write today's class goals on the board, and I busy myself setting out our teaching books. A number of students run up to me demanding to see what stickers are available today for those brave enough to raise their hands in front of everyone. I smile, show them the options, and listen to the chatter. I'm on good terms with this group of twenty-eight kids, but it does little to soothe my worries.

Class 1-4 has already defeated one English teacher, and I witnessed every painful battle. Ito Sensei is our rescue force. I trust him completely, but part of me is worried that even Ito Sensei, tamer of teens and enforcer of the English language, is going to fail here.

This class is a volatile combination of large personalities and damaged hearts. Among this group of kids are those with behavior disorders, learning disabilities, broken homes, friend problems, and all of the above. When the incoming freshmen were split into four home-rooms, the teachers had no way of knowing if the class dimensions would work. In this case, just about everything has gone wrong.

We've cleared the opening minutes of class and are introducing today's new grammar concept when a hand shoots up in the middle of the room. I look at the boy with his hand raised, and I tense up. Here it comes.

"Ito Sensei, I'm sick, I'm gonna go to the nurse's office." He doesn't even bother to sound ill. His name is Akira. A tall, good-looking kid, he's faster, stronger, and more streetwise than most of his yearmates. He's smart too, but the teachers aren't sure how smart because he refuses to hand in homework or focus on tests. At the beginning of the year, there were high hopes that Akira would be one of the leaders and help rein in some of his rowdier classmates. Instead he joined forces with them.

My grandfather, a teacher for more than forty years, said that you can always tell what kind of student a kid is going to be by the friends he chooses. I've found this to be true most of the time, but in the case of this particular young man, it doesn't quite hold. Akira runs with the bad kids during the day, but he's a star of the tight-knit, clean-cut baseball team too. He jokes around with the louder, irreverent girls but counts some of the quietest, nicest girls as his friends. I know his mother, a kind woman who always makes time to talk to the American teacher.

His father is dead.

Now Ito Sensei meets his gaze. "Do you have a fever?"

"Nah."

"Does your stomach hurt?"

"No, I'm gonna go see the nurse." His friends snicker as he stands up and heads toward the door.

"Sit down." Ito Sensei's voice is a bit louder than usual. "I think you can endure the last thirty minutes of class." Akira has stopped halfway to the door. "Sit down," Ito Sensei says again and watches as the young man does so, amid the alert silence of the class. "Good, let's continue."

I'm impressed. The previous teacher would have been happy to let this student spend the entire semester in the nurse's office. Ito Sensei has apparently decided to try a different tactic. I turn toward the board, when a sudden gasp from the girls makes me whirl back around.

I'm not sure what's going on until I see the blood. Somehow Akira has managed to give himself a bloody nose. Having suffered a fair share of bloody noses as a child thanks to bad sinuses, I know that they are relatively easy to start—a hard knock on the nose is all it takes. They are also usually easy to stop, but this doesn't seem to be Akira's goal. Instead he's rubbing the bridge of his nose, exacerbating the flow.

Ito Sensei continues teaching. I'm frozen, as are most of the students. One of the girls offers the boy some tissues, but he throws them on the floor. I glance at Ito Sensei, unsure of what to do, but he keeps going, so I follow along. Akira starts shaking his head, spattering his desk with blood droplets. His friends are gazing at him with a mixture of concern and awe. The muttering grows.

Ito Sensei finally stops his lecture and looks at the boy. "You've got a bloody nose?"

A terse nod.

"If you need ice to stop it, you may go to the nurse's office."

The sheer rage in Akira's face chills me.

"Nah, I'm fine." The other boys in the class are nearly beside themselves at this show of contempt. He has managed to move up a level in their rebel ranking.

Ito Sensei does nothing more than nod and return to the lesson. I'm getting queasy looking at all the blood. Some of it has gotten on

Akira's hands, and he smears it on his desk and white shirt. There's some on his cheek. He hits his desk with his fist, and his textbooks fall to the floor with a clatter. I pick them up and place them carefully on the corner of his desk. Not even glancing in my direction, he sweeps them to the floor. I back off.

My hands are shaking. The last fifteen minutes of class feel like fifty.

By the end of the hour, Ito Sensei is as serene as he was at the beginning. I am near tears. The students sweep out, surrounding their classmate and leaving us alone in the classroom with the blood-smeared desk.

After depositing my teaching materials in the teachers' room, I grab a water bottle and almost run out to the school grounds. *I need air, I need to think, I've had enough.* Out in the corner of the schoolyard, under the low-hanging Shinto-god branches, is the little jizo shrine I uncovered the first week of school. Refilling his small offering cup with water, I crouch down before the jizo statue and try to clear my head.

I had a happy childhood—sitcom-level happy. I had two loving parents, a sister who was and still is my best friend, two doting grandparents living in the attached house, another set who owned a magical farm, and a fluffy dog that chased after rabbits and squirrels in the yard. I had my moments of adolescent anger but never to the extent that I just witnessed. Then again, I can't even begin to imagine how hard it must be for a young boy to lose his father at the age he needs him the most.

But to smear blood all over yourself? Just to disturb English class?

Logically, I know his anger is deep, consuming, and not related to anything that happened in our classroom. But how does one even begin to heal such hurt? As often happens in the moments I have no idea how to deal with, I start praying. The prayer on my lips is my favorite and most used: the prayer to my guardian angel. As a child I found it too intimidating to pray to God directly. Instead I prayed to my guardian angel. Now is no different.

"Angel of God, my guardian dear. To whom God's love commits me here. Ever this day be at my side, to light, to guard, to rule, to guide." I breathe.

It occurs to me that in a Buddhist sense, Ojizo-sama is a guardian angel. In my weekly trips out here, I have, in fact, gained a Japanese version of the angel I've always had. When I was younger and worried about my dad on his long business trips, I would often pray to my angel to be with him and offer some extra protection. Facing my little stone Buddha, I decide to try it out.

"Ojizo-sama, can you help this boy? I don't know what to do, but just protect him more, please."

My prayers said, I stand up and walk back to the school building. It's lunchtime, and as the students rush around getting ready, I head slowly back toward the teachers' room. I have to pass the nurse's office to get there, and as I approach, Akira exits, surrounded by his friends. Deciding it's better to say something than to stay silent, I call his name. "Are you okay? You scared me."

His friends jostle him playfully. "Hey, you scared Ellen Sensei, you idiot!"

He stops, and a friendly smile crosses the face that was twisted in anger only minutes before. "I'm okay. Sorry 'bout that."

I smile back, and he and his gang move on.

Eyes lowered, avoiding any more human contact, I go to my desk to fetch my chopsticks. Better to eat alone in the backroom today—I've exceeded my daily allowance of teenage mood swings.

I don't know what kind of divine link Ojizo-sama has, but I'm going to keep refilling his water cup.

13

Prayer and Parenting

Jane

*Every person understands God in some small measure.
Being satisfied with that small measure is idolatry.*
—Juris Rubenis, Latvian pastor, author of
Finding God in a Tangled World

For years, Dean and I prayed the rosary with our two daughters, paid the Catholic school tuition, volunteered for the fundraisers, doled out the straw for the crèche one strand at a time, and shook their sullen teenage hands during the sign of peace. At the same time, I team-taught Lutheran Sunday school and helped out with the vacation Bible programs every summer. Dean was the cantor on Sundays with the Lutherans and the pianist at the all-school Mass on Fridays at St. Monica School.

Would all of that lead Ellen and Martha to have faith in God? I doubted it was enough, so I put in some worry to push the scales over the tipping point. I scowled at the vampire novels and talked up the church youth group. This worked about as well as one would expect.

When Ellen first left home for college, I tried not to panic that this would bring about the end of regular Sunday Mass attendance. She still went to church with us on Christmas and Easter. *That's pretty good*, I told myself, but I fretted that it wasn't a passing grade. My grade, not hers. Faith is not something that comes from people; it is a gift from

God, but someone has to teach the basics of the tradition. Someone also has to support the community of believers who pass on the traditions. When Ellen missed church, it felt like a rejection of the community, and it felt like my fault. I had received this wonderful inheritance, my faith tradition, and I had failed to pass it on to the next generation. My strangely transferable guilt had a stunting effect on conversations between us about either faith or God.

I compared notes with a friend who also had college-age offspring.

"Do you worry about Mark's faith?" I asked.

"Yes," she answered with furrowed brow. "He might not go into the monastery after all. He met a girl at the World Youth Day last summer. It looks like they may get married."

I did not see the issue—marriage is a sacrament, right? What did my friend have to worry about? But if she was stressed, it was a huge affirmation of my own angst.

Now Ellen lives in a place where even my guilt can't reach her.

St. Francis Xavier, one of the first Jesuits, traveled to Japan, and even though he didn't survive the trip, the Catholic faith did. In fact, he made so many converts among the Japanese population that it annoyed the establishment—a sure sign of zeal if ever there was one. There must be vestiges of Catholicism floating around somewhere in that country.

But this jizo shrine she is tending brings me at last to the moment when I realize that worry isn't cutting it anymore. Could it be that it's not possible to worry a child back into the faith community? Especially if that child is two hours from a Catholic church and fourteen hours by jet plane away from the sight of my frustrated and overheated face?

Jesus said, "Ask and it will be given to you." He didn't say, "Bite your nails and lie awake at night."

So, in place of that, I fold a holy card inside my next letter.

Ellen writes back an e-mail about climbing mountains to visit Shinto shrines and staying up all night on her birthday to honor the dead in Buddhist cemeteries. Everyone in Japan, it seems, is both Shinto, an ancient animist religion, and Buddhist. But they also admire some Christian traditions—lace wedding dresses and nondenominational wedding chapels are especially popular.

Hence the modern proverb: *Born Shinto, marry Christian, die Buddhist.*

She tells about praying at dawn in a Buddhist monastery and how the monks struck the backs of meditating devotees with long sticks in order to help them reach a deeper awareness. "They didn't hit me very hard because I was a foreigner," she writes with disappointment.

The holy card goes unremarked—by both of us.

Instead, I start a novena to St. Francis Xavier. The nine days of prayer are transformative for me; unlike worry, this prayer has a clearly defined beginning and ending. It becomes not so much fretting as it is a vigilant focus. Nine days is an interesting stretch of prayer: long enough to make the effort feel substantial, but not so long that I become obsessive about it. And then it is finished.

Worry is never finished. Prayer isn't either, but it has restful places, such as candle lighting.

Lighting candles is becoming my favorite way not to worry. I walk into the empty church any time of day, slip some coins into the slot, strike a match, genuflect, bless myself, maybe kneel down for a few Hail Marys, and I am on my way. It takes care of the problem on my mind in both a concrete and spiritual way and saves a ton of money—no anti-anxiety drugs, no retail therapy, and no long-distance phone calls to Japan.

Another of my new discoveries is to change the way I say the rosary. I start to use the beads to count blessings instead of counting troubles.

It becomes a gratitude prayer instead of a "now and at the hour of our death" sort of thing.

As my children become adults, my role is changing. It is transforming slowly into a pause to watch God work on my daughters' faith, instead of anxiously trying to shape it myself. This isn't obedience. It is another way to practice my religion. This feels something like that way of life Jesus hints at when he talks about the Holy Spirit.

During autumn, on Facebook, I hover in the wings while Ellen describes a pilgrimage to the ancient religious site at Kyoto where she burned incense, washed her hands in ceremonial fountains, and purchased prayer beads from the shrine maidens.

"It's just like the holy water and the rosaries that our teachers used to give us," she writes.

I slip a St. Christopher medal into the next care package.

I pray regularly all during Advent. Christmas becomes not so much about parties and gifts, but more about longing for a sign that my daughter is not as out of God's reach as she is out of mine. This is something new, anyway. Even if Ellen isn't getting any more Christian, at least I am.

One day, halfway through December, she thanks me for sending the new Miraculous Medals, and asks me to light a candle for a friend. "I guess we're both feeling a little homesick because of missing the holidays."

"That might be it," I say, suppressing the urge for details.

"Yesterday, some of the junior high girls saw my St. Christopher medal and said, 'Is that a *real* Christian medal?' I told them it was, but part of my contract stipulates that I am not allowed to evangelize, so I didn't explain it to them. They wanted to see it close-up, so I took it off and they passed it all around. Isn't that funny?"

"Hmm."

"Would you send me a couple more of those medals? My friends might like them."

"Sure thing."

"And don't forget to have Father Mike bless them."

I am a longtime volunteer at the St. Vincent de Paul thrift store in my town. In this humble little shop, I have learned to look for God around every corner and inside every soul. The people who hang out at the shop have cracked open a hole in my spirit that doesn't want to heal. And that's okay.

One day at the store, I am listening to an elderly gentleman tell me about his troubles trying to find the money to cover his electric bill. He broke his budget to pay for his nephew's funeral. It is a privilege to be of assistance in these situations.

I begin by offering my condolences, and he nods and says, "You gotta give a person a flower while they can still smell. I did what I could for my nephew when he was alive, so I have no regrets. He's in a good place now. Jesus has him."

Sitting up straight, I am listening closely because he is telling me that I already gave my flowers to Ellen. So often I find my true spiritual teachers in the disguises of the poor. I smile slowly at him.

He grins back. "Jesus is coming back, you know? And he's gonna bust a cloud open with that book of his."

This time I laugh. "You have a lot of wisdom."

He shrugs. "It would be sad if God kept me on the earth this long and I couldn't tell you nothing."

"Is it all right if I tell other people what you know?"

"Sure it's all right, especially the part about him coming back."

I assist my teacher with a promissory note for his electric bill, and we part after praying together. So beautiful and so simple, this sharing of faith and love and prayer. Why is it so difficult with my own daughter? Why can a near-stranger confide in me that "Jesus is coming back," and yet I hesitate to say such things to Ellen?

Like this gentleman, I think it's sad that God keeps me on the earth this long, and yet I feel helpless to tell the people I love what God has shown me.

Then the phone call comes that I had given up as hopeless. Loyola Press, a Jesuit publisher in Chicago, wants to talk about the thrift-store book. After years of submissions and rejection letters, and nearly giving up the whole idea, the book about the people I've met in the thrift store has been accepted.

Prayer and worry are not the same thing at all. I am beginning to understand that they are opposites.

14

Christmas

Jane

Christmas is not the same. Ellen, obviously, is too far away to come home, and even if she wanted to spend the thousands of dollars on the holiday-rate airline ticket, she would need to ask for too many days off from work.

At the end of our long, traditional dinner, while my sister, sisters-in-law, and I are cleaning up the kitchen, Dean, Martha, and a couple of the girls' cousins, Will and Ian, are Skyping with her at the kitchen table.

"What did you do for Christmas?" Martha asks. "Did you find someone to celebrate with?"

"Yesterday was a regular school day here, so I worked at the elementary school up in the mountains all morning. We played a game I invented to help them learn about the American holidays. It's a quiz game called 'Panda or Santa?'"

I'm intrigued, and even though I am up to my wrists in soapy water, I ask, "They don't know the difference?"

"Well, pandas and Santas have more in common than you may think. Sample: *I climb trees—am I Panda or Santa?* Or: *I climb houses—Panda? Or Santa?* And: *I eat cookies—Panda? Or Santa?* That one was tough because who doesn't like cookies?"

Her cousin Will looks at the brightly decorated Christmas cookie in his hand and says, "Exactly. Did you make Christmas cookies?"

"I couldn't because there is no oven in a Japanese kitchen, but I gobbled up all the ones my mom sent in the mail. The Japanese have a tradition of eating KFC on Christmas. They think it is an American holiday, so they eat American food."

"What?" I protest. "It's a religious holiday—not an *American* holiday!"

"Yeah, but not so much here in Japan. Christmas is all about dating and colored lights, and the very worst Christmas songs ever invented. If I hear 'Rockin' around the Christmas Tree' one more time, I might just run screaming from the store. But Christmas evening was okay. Some of us expats went to a karaoke parlor together to sing some carols. We had fun."

"Who was there?" I ask. "Robin, Rodger?"

"They both live too far away, and besides, Rodger went home for a visit. Actually, I was kind of surprised he could get the time off since we've been here for only four months. Some of the local JETs and ALTs came: Ayden, he's from New Zealand; Mark, from Hawaii; people from England, Scotland—it was interesting finding which carols we had in common."

Martha asks if she received our Christmas package, which she affirms with effusive gratitude.

"My students loved the stickers you sent, but I ate all the chocolate myself. Is that bad? It made me homesick to see all the holiday cookies and candy, so I didn't tell any of my friends."

Martha laughs. "It's not bad. Did you listen to the CD yet?"

"It's in my car—love, love, love it."

The fuzzy video and delayed response make the conversation awkward at times. The Skype website is setting records in the number of people online tonight. The cousins wander off to the living room to play a new board game. Ellen's aunts and uncles pop into camera range for a minute of holiday wishes and then go back to their conversations. We finish the dishes, and I sit down to chat, but it is time for Ellen to get ready for work. "I'll call you in your morning," she tells me. "Merry Christmas, everyone!"

Christmas just isn't the same.

15

Rodger

Ellen

It's a bitterly cold January day in Kotoura, and I am huddled one foot away from one of the kerosene stoves that ring the teachers' room. Japanese architecture, famed as it is for its simplicity and clean lines, is designed largely for the purpose of keeping out the suffocating heat of summer. Corridors and rooms are aligned to funnel their own cooling breezes, and every wall features large windows.

As brilliant as this design is for the hottest months, it creates misery in the winter. With next to no insulation and without the benefit of central heating, it's not unusual to see one's breath when walking between classrooms. Both teachers and children wear multiple layers of clothing, resorting to heat packs that can be stuck to any part of the body.

I'm a Michigan child. I've grown up with cool summers and snow-bound winters. School can be canceled because of wind chill alone. But even for a rugged northern girl like me, Tottori winters suck. The only way to escape the cold completely is to submerge oneself in the nearby town of Misasa's famed hot spring baths and wait there until spring. Alas, I'm expected to report to school five days a week and must limit simmering in the baths to the weekends.

Once my hands are reddened by the stove's irregular flame, I rush to the locker room to slip on gloves, coat, and hat. I don't spend as many long hours at school in the winter. Though I might like the company, I prefer being able to huddle unapologetically under my **quilted heating table** (called a *kotatsu*) at home, sipping hot tea and dreaming of August.

When I get home, I go through the regular procedure: put water on to boil, turn on the kotatsu coils, close the sliding walls into my living room, and plug in my computer. If I'm going to be stuck in one position for the rest of the evening, I plan on watching reruns of *So You Think You Can Dance* online.

Before watching reality TV, I check in with my other purveyor of real-life drama: Facebook. Today nothing seems particularly out of order on my newsfeed. It's the usual posts: pictures of my friends' dinners, videos of cats, and complaints about the weather. I'm about to log off when one comment on a status catches my eye: "WTH?! This is a sick joke to play on someone, guys!"

Genuine emotion pulses through those letters. I click on it to reveal the entire message thread. It starts with a status posted on one of my friend's pages: "Rodger passed away yesterday. Please keep him and his family in your prayers."

Surely this can't be right.

In seconds I'm opening home pages, checking other friends' statuses, looking for the post in which the punch line will be revealed and everyone will take a moment to yell at the prankster in caps lock. But there isn't one. This must be real. But . . . how?

Rodger is not one of my closest friends, but our lives have run parallel for so long that he is, in a strange way, my life-path twin. Both of us are Michiganders, raised in happy families in small towns. We attended the same university and ended up in the same classes. After studying Japanese together, we decided to study abroad at the same time. Though we went to different programs, we returned to America the same month and once again found ourselves enrolled in the same final courses before graduating in the same ceremony.

Though I had planned on working in the States after graduation, the faltering economy caused me to look to Japan for employment. Rodger, on the other hand, had planned to be an ESL (English as a Second Language) teacher, and thus, once again, we found ourselves applying for the same job opportunities. As it turned out, we were both accepted, and even carpooled to our orientation together. The morning we flew from Detroit to Tokyo, our parents stood next to each other at the airport and exchanged nervous chitchat as we checked our bags at the counter. Our dads even stepped in to take pictures for each other's families during the final farewell.

Rodger's placement put him far in the north of Japan, whereas I was sent to Tottori, but thanks to Rodger's popular YouTube vlogs, I was able to check in on him frequently and follow his progress in settling into life in a rural town similar to mine.

Rodger is a true gentleman. A huge fan of George Michael's music and Japanese films, he is also a budding translator, recently blogging about his mission to translate one of his favorite poets for an English audience.

He seemed happy and healthy in the last video, so how could this be true?

After some frantic Internet searching and a few harried inquiries, I have my answer. It's real. It was a tragic, freak stomach ailment. Rodger woke up with a stomachache and passed away later the same day. A friend who had driven him to the hospital was now in charge of alerting his family, whom Rodger had just visited for the holidays.

I, too, am stuck with the task of making a phone call to one of our mutual Japanese friends I recently visited. We had been talking at the time of getting everyone together over the summer, but now . . .

It's a horrible, raw phone call. My Japanese fails me halfway through, and I start to cry, which is what really alerts my friend to the true meaning behind my words. He's in denial, and I don't have the strength to listen to his grief over the phone. I apologize, promise to call later, and hang up.

I call the person I always call when I'm crying: my mom. She listens, reacts, says all the words about heaven and eternal life that I thought I wanted to hear. But it's not working. If anything, I'm getting more upset, and I realize with a start that she is not the person I can talk to about this.

I can't talk to her because, for the first time in my life, I can't tell her what I'm afraid of. It won't come out, whether because of my own panic or because I realize telling her will only make this worse.

It's a Thursday night, I have a seminar the next day, and I really should not go anywhere, but I absolutely can't be alone right now. I send a frantic text to Ayden, asking if he has some time to talk. He replies that he's got an English conversation class until seven, but if I want to come over after that, it's cool.

It will take me less than twenty-five minutes to drive there, and the clock says 6:10, but I leave immediately. Even if it means waiting in my car in the parking lot outside his building, I'd prefer that to sitting in front of this computer screen with its steadily increasing message chain of shared sadness.

Ayden pulls in when he said he would, tired but cheerful after a long day of multiple classes. He trots over to my car and plops down in the passenger seat. "Hey gorgeous, how're you handling your amazingness?"

My smile feels stretched. "Fine. I'm fine."

He's half-started on a story about one of his students when he realizes what I said and turns to look at me fully. "Fine? No one says 'fine' except second-language learners and people who aren't." My eyes start to tear up, so he opens the door and motions for me to follow. "C'mon, I've got an electric carpet and some tea upstairs."

By the time I'm wrapped in a blanket and seated on the warming carpet, the tears are back full force. The story comes pouring out, and Ayden listens silently as he shuffles around the kitchen. When I reach the part about texting him, he joins me in the small living room, pulling the sliding partition shut to block out the draft. He hands me a cup of tea, a box of tissues, and some chocolates. "They've got brandy in the middle," he informs me. "Better eat them all."

But the tissues are the first thing I grab. "It's just so horrible," I sob, not even trying to censor myself anymore. "It was so fast!"

"Yeah, that's—"

I can't stop. The true fear, the part I couldn't tell my mom, comes gasping out. "But he was alone! He died in Japan, and his family wasn't here. There wasn't anyone there who loved him." I can't go on.

It's the one fear that no preparation can soothe or fix.

Ayden is silent. He takes a chocolate for himself, pushes my tea closer to me, and thinks. I sniffle and wait. I don't even know what I'm waiting for. My mother already told me all the platitudes that reinforce the afterlife I've been raised to believe. But it didn't help. So here I am waiting for this man, who doesn't even believe in heaven, to fill this gaping tear that has been ripped into my faith.

"You're wrong," he says finally, "about him being alone."

I shake my head. "I know there were doctors, and his friend was there, but I meant—"

Ayden cuts me off. "I know what you meant. You think people who really loved him, really knew him were far away. But that's wrong." He leans forward. "Everything you told me about this guy, what he was doing, what kind of a teacher he was . . . it's obvious he was loved. Not only that, but it sounds like he was *doing* what he loved, he was being the person he'd always wanted to be."

"But—"

"And," Ayden continues, "you said yourself that he was in a town a lot like Kotoura. What would Kotoura do if *you* died? Do you think you'd be without love? Do you think they don't know you here? Be serious, Knuth—they'd fall apart. Think about his students. Poor kids."

Oh. We stare at each other for several seconds before Ayden grabs my teacup and stands. "I'll get you a fill-up. I was serious about eating those chocolates by the way, but if you eat more than five you might have to spend the night. You know how crazy strict the cops are about alcohol."

Obediently, I grab a chocolate and unwrap it. It's bitter, and the brandy burns my tongue, but it suits my mood. I lay my pounding head on my knees and listen to Ayden move around the kitchen. Love, I think, is a funny thing. I'm always thinking about it.

What am I missing?

16

I'll Call You in Your Morning

Jane

Dean has just left for work, and I'm cleaning up the breakfast dishes when the phone rings. The display tells me that it is a Skype caller, so I answer, "Good evening, Ellen!"

"Hi, Ma. Do you have to be anywhere this morning? I need to talk."

I turn off the running water in the sink and sit down at the table. "What's up? I've got plenty of time."

The story of Rodger's sudden death spills out. Ellen is crying and anxious. I try to soothe her with sympathetic words, but what I want to give her is a long hug.

I need one from her too. Rodger was the young man at the airport who flew off to Japan on the same flight with Ellen. I remember his excitement, his laughter . . . and his family. We snapped photos of him and his parents.

His mother. I remember meeting his mother.

As Ellen tells me of her shock and grief, all I can think about is Rodger's mother getting a phone call from a hospital in Japan. This is truly awful.

For the first time since Ellen left, I don't want my daughter to be pursuing this dream of hers anymore. I want her to come home, or at least, closer to home. I not only can't hug her, I can't seem to comfort her in any way at all. She doesn't want to hear about faith and the eternal existence of Rodger's soul. And frankly, I can't find comfort in talking about ultimate things either.

It's not that I doubt my faith. I don't doubt God's goodness. I know that Rodger, a truly good person, is safe in God's arms. I'm not worried about Rodger. My thoughts veer toward Rodger's mother and father. Theirs is the heartache that crushes me. This could have happened to my daughter. At this moment, it's the ones left behind who are not safe. And Ellen is one of them.

I want to hold Ellen. But I can't do that, and my words are not enough. She is simply too far away. This is the moment when the faith I have tried so hard to pass on to her is not helping like I want it to help. I feel like a failure.

Listening to her sobs, I hear myself telling her to find someone else. "Is there a friend you can call, honey? It would be better if you meet up with Claire or Mark or Ayden—it's not good if you try to take all this to bed with you tonight. Please, tell me that you'll go talk with someone."

Gulping back her tears, she agrees that her apartment is not a friendly place right now. She promises me that she will call someone. More sympathy, more pledges to pray for Rodger and his family, and a simple blessing for her over the phone.

"I'll call you in your morning," I promise her.

When I hang up, the sunrise is streaming in the living room windows, but that only means it is night in Japan. I am a failed child of God.

God, on the other hand, uses failures almost exclusively. This is true. It's in the Bible.

17

Commandments

Ellen

I am standing in the checkout line at the supermarket, (always a prime place for being approached by curious local residents. *Look! The English teacher eats bananas!*) when a gentle cough alerts me to incoming conversation.

"Excuse me, so sorry, but you are the English teacher?" A petite older woman is standing behind me holding a basket full of fresh produce. She has a gentle, oval face creased by a nervous smile.

"Yes, I'm Ellen, it's nice to meet you." We take a few seconds to bow to each other. "And you are . . .?"

"My name is Kodani," she says in rushed but clear English. "I'm so happy to see you."

"Oh! You speak English very well!" My compliment makes her blush, and she switches back to Japanese.

"No, no, no, I don't, but I want to study it more."

"That's great!"

She peers at me expectantly.

"Um . . . where do you study?" I ask.

"Oh, at your nighttime English class!" She rushes to elaborate, "Of course, you haven't taught it yet, but it's yours."

"I have a nighttime English class?" This is new to me. "When is it?"

"Every Tuesday night." Kodani's laugh is as gentle as her bearing. "It is volunteer I'm afraid, we can't pay you. But we do bring you dinner because we know it is so late and such a difficult imposition . . ."

"Did the previous ALT do this too?" I ask, wondering what kind of "voluntary" we are talking about.

"So sorry, yes she did. And the ALT before her. All the ALTs for the past ten years, actually."

Ah, that kind of voluntary.

Thus begins my adventures with teaching English classes in Manabi town center. I'm not a stellar teacher by anyone's estimation. Most of my energy is used up earlier in the day during my contractually obligated job, and I often come up with conversation topics on the fly, improvising a "grammar point of the day" as we go.

But the students are wonderful, and thanks to their dedication and kindness, Tuesday nights are often a high point in my week. Now, as I rush down the third-floor corridor and into our usual room, they all greet me cheerfully, as if I'm not five minutes late.

I drop into my chair at the head of the room and start off with the usual pleasantries, checking to see how many participants have shown up on this blustery night. Our class has a core group of five members who never miss a week, though this week two of our satellite members have driven in.

The students are a fun, random gathering: 80 percent women, 50 percent mothers of my current students, 30 percent retired housewives, and 20 percent young professionals hoping to take English-ranking tests to improve their standing in the job market. Language-ability level varies widely, but the stronger students help the weaker ones during activities, and no one would dream of belittling someone for making a mistake.

Most of the time our serious, grammar-focused activities take wide detours into general discussions about the differences between countries, cultures, and beliefs—and men. Bored housewives love to talk about love, celebrities, and relationships. As the youngest and the only single one in the group, I usually defer to their more informed opinions. Usually.

Today my daily grammar point is handed to me as one of them struggles with the contraction *should* and *not*. I stand up to write the correct English on the whiteboard behind me, and they dutifully pull out pens and paper to take notes. We review the meaning of *should* and *shouldn't* for the students who are slightly behind. As I take a seat, the most advanced student in the class speaks up.

"What is the difference between *should* and *shall?*"

Sometimes her questions are too difficult for me to answer, she's that well-studied. Luckily, I know the answer to this one. "*Should* is more of a suggestion, something you are obligated to do or not do. *Shall* is future tense, something that you will or will not do. It's more definite."

"I often hear you use *should*, but not *shall*, why is that?"

Drat. I chew the inside of my cheek while I think. "Well . . . I guess *shall* is kind of older English. We don't use it so much anymore. You see it more in writing . . ."

"Like what?" They peer at me curiously, pens poised.

"Um, that's a good question. I guess in declarations or . . . or . . . rules." My mind's temporary blankness suddenly dissipates. "Oh! Like in the Bible, the Ten Commandments. You know? Like: 'Thou shall not kill.'"

"What? The Bible?" Before I can explain, the mother of two of my elementary students clarifies.

"The book which tells Christians that they can't eat octopus."

"Christians can't eat octopus? Really?" Their mouths drop open in astonishment. "But, Ellen, *you* eat octopus."

"I, well, yes. Only really conservative Christian groups still believe that," I say. "Catholics don't follow it word for word, they interpret the—."

"But these commandment rules—you follow them exactly?"

I'm losing ground fast. "Well, yes, but they're a little different."

"How are they different?"

"Well, because God said them."

"God did not say you shall not eat octopus?"

I can't even remember which Old Testament book that particular part was written in. "I . . . I don't know who said that exactly . . ."

"Hmm . . ." They're skeptical. Any god who thinks one of Japan's go-to proteins is "unclean" is undeniably suspicious.

I decide to get the conversation back on track by talking louder. "Soooo, anyway, the Ten Commandments are ten rules that Christians have to follow so we can go to heaven."

Blessedly, they leave the octopus proclamation alone. "What happens if you don't follow them?"

"If we don't apologize for what we did or if we break them a lot, we might end up in hell."

"Wow!" They are suitably impressed. "What are these rules?"

I stand back up to write them on the board. "There are easy and hard ones," I explain. "For example, 'You shall not say the name of God in vain.'" I hasten to explain the difficult English, "That basically means, you shouldn't say 'God' or 'Oh my God!' unless you're actually praying or calling to him."

"Really?" Thanks to movies, "oh my god" is one of the English phrases that Japanese students of all ages know how to say. "You're not supposed to say that?"

"No, not really." I'm about to continue but stop at the look on one woman's face. "What's wrong?"

"Does this mean Tom Cruise will go to hell?" she asks worriedly. "He often says 'oh my god.'"

Uh oh. "Not if he's really sorry for it . . ." To avoid this becoming an impassioned discussion on the state of Tom Cruise's soul, I hurry on to the next commandment. "Another would be: 'You shall respect your father and mother.'"

This is widely decreed as a good rule, and we manage to get the other eight rules up on the board in short order. I have to look up the last one on my phone: "Thou shall observe the Sabbath day and keep it holy." Probably best not to mention to my mother that I forgot that one . . .

They copy down the rules for successful admission into heaven, chattering back and forth over words that some know and others don't. One of them raises a hand. "Excuse me, Ellen, but what does the word 'adultery' mean?"

"Good question!" I tap the whiteboard with the marker. "Adultery means cheating on your husband or wife."

"Oh." Most of them nod immediately, but the same woman has another question. "But what if you just kiss them?"

"Uh . . ." I've never really thought about it. "I think it's just sex."

"What kind of sex? All kinds of sex?" Now a few more women are nodding. "What if you just think about it?" asks another.

"Most of the time, if you're thinking about it, you're already breaking this rule." I point out "You Shall Not Covet." "So you should probably avoid both."

"That's impossible!" a young teacher argues. "Everyone thinks those things!"

She's right; it looks like we're all going to hell with Tom Cruise. "Yes, but if you're sorry for it and sincerely regret your actions, God will forgive you," I remind them. "And it's easier to ask forgiveness for just thinking something than for killing someone, for example."

"How many times will he forgive you?" someone wants to know.

"As many times as you're really sorry." I waggle my finger at them. "But you have to try to do better."

Several different discussions spring up, and another question comes my way. "How many commandments have you broken, Ellen?"

It's been awhile since I blushed. Awesome, good to know those blood vessels still work. "Er . . . well . . . enough . . ."

"And are you very sorry?"

"Usually?"

"But how does your god know that?"

"Well, he can see my heart," I say, finally confident in an answer. "He always knows what I'm thinking."

They gasp in horror. "He can see your heart? How embarrassing! Can you imagine? Ellen, are you okay with that?"

"Yes?"

"But perhaps he will be angry about the octopus you've eaten!"

This conversation is lost. I sigh and sit down. "Let's have our tea break, shall we?" For the first time in years, I feel like maybe I should go to confession. Stupid octopus.

18

Thrift Store Saints

Jane

The book is finally published. *Thrift Store Saints: Meeting Jesus 25 Cents at a Time* has come out in paperback with a charming cover and generous readers. I am as busy and as happy as one would think I would be. It is a delightful, humbling, focused, and confusing time, and I love it. I want to share this joy with everyone in my life, and almost everyone is there to celebrate with me.

Except Ellen, of course.

That's okay. That's how it's supposed to be. Children grow up and move away, and they make their own lives.

I send her a signed copy in a slim package and wait the ten days to hear if she received it. On Facebook she posts a photo of herself holding up the book for the camera and adds lavish, congratulatory praise for the content.

The next Saturday morning, on Skype, I can't wait to hear from her personally about what she thinks of the spiritual journey her mother has unfolded in the small volume. "You liked it?" I ask, knowing full well she can't really say anything but "yes."

"Yeah," she answers, smiling. "Great job, Ma. Of course, I knew a lot of the stories already, so there weren't many surprises."

"Of course, sure." No surprises? I pretty much spilled my entire spiritual awakening in those stories.

She can sense my hidden disappointment. I can see from the expression on her face that she is trying hard to think of something else to say. "The time compression was kind of weird. Some of those stories took place when we were little, and some happened last year, so that bothered me while I was reading. But other than that, it was great."

"I'm sorry I only sent you one copy. I should have sent more."

"Oh, no problem. I can order it if I need another. I might do that for my friend Mark. I think he might like it. I'm sure he will." She is being kind.

I received a similar reaction from my students. Eighth graders are not extremely interested in geometry, but math problems trump thrift-store enlightenment any day.

I wonder why I thought I needed to write. Neither my daughter nor my students seem to find much that is interesting in my simple stories. My family and friends have heard all these stories before. Have I been delusional about this?

How hard it is to hear God speak, to feel his light touch, his gentle direction. It makes me wonder if I have anything more to give.

Give silence. Listen. Learn.

Yes. There is always silence to give. Perhaps now is the time to give that gift to my daughter—and to seek out her gifts.

"So . . . what's going on in Tohaku?" I ask the kind, uncertain face on my computer screen.

19

Lambs and Dragons

Ellen

It's August 13, two days before my birthday. The humidity of the Japanese summer has hit, bringing with it the incessant buzz of the cicadas and the full-body perspiration that I keep trying to convince myself is good for my pores. Today also marks the start of the three-day Bon Festival, one of Japan's oldest national holidays that is also called the Buddhist Festival of the Dead.

My birthday happens to be the climax of the three-day period of solemn remembrance. Birthday party? Nope, sorry, this is family time, a time to gather and remember those who have passed on. Meet for coffee? Only if you don't mind meeting at McDonald's, every other restaurant is sure to be closed. Drinks after dinner? Not unless you want to sit with everyone else in town in the graveyard with a candle lit to guide grandpa's soul home.

I've already resigned myself to another birthday spent enjoying a pile of Kit Kat bars purchased at the local convenience store. Not just any Kit Kats. Special limited-edition, summer mango flavor! I have tentative plans to meet some foreign friends at the beach. Not the beach by the large graveyard though. Running around in swimsuits while our Japanese neighbors clean their family graves would be gauche.

I have, however, extended myself the luxury of three days off work. I have weeks of unused vacation time, having fallen accustomed to the Japanese habit of never taking a day off. I'm not sure how much of this is genetic—my dad is a bit of a workaholic—and how much is wanting to fit in with my coworkers. No one wants to be the only one absent on Christmas—how irresponsible.

My first day of vacation is going great. It's ten in the morning, and I'm still in my pajamas, sprawled on the woven straw mats that cover the floor of my living/bed/dining room. After about twenty minutes of contemplation, I decide I should probably change the burned-out light bulb in the main lamp sometime before winter. No rush though.

My Japanese cell phone sparkles to life, chirping cheerfully just out of arm's reach. I consider ignoring it, but sigh and roll over toward it, picking up on the fourth ring.

"Hello?"

"Hello, Ellen Sensei, this is Mr. Okamoto from Tohaku Junior High."

Vice Principal Okamoto? I bolt upright to check my calendar. It's really August 13, right? I'm certain I asked for this day off. I even got the approval form stamped by Mr. Okamoto, Principal Ishiga, and my town office supervisor. Did I forget to tell someone? Did I use the wrong stamp again? "Good morning, Vice Principal Okamoto . . ."

"Good morning, Ellen Sensei, where are you right now?"

When in doubt, start with an apology. "Oh, I'm sorry, I'm at my apartment. I was planning to use my vacation time today, you see—."

"Your apartment in Tokuman neighborhood? Oh good. Do you have time this morning?"

I relax a little. There has been no instant censor or condemnation. Maybe I did use the right stamp. "Er, well, yes. I'm not busy. Has something come up at school?" I'm racking my brain, trying to remember if I forgot to do something important. It's summer vacation though, and the only assigned thing I've done in the past two weeks is teach a swim class to the preschoolers down the street.

"Nothing at school, no. I was wondering if you'd like to come to the funeral-supply store with me."

I can honestly say that no one has ever asked me to go to a funeral-supply store before. I must not give off that "enjoys picking out headstones" vibe.

"The . . . funeral-supply store?"

From Vice Principal Okamoto's tone I can tell he finds my hesitation unexpected. "Why yes, I thought maybe you'd like to go pick out a new offering cup for the jizo statue you're taking care of. I have to go myself to buy incense for my family graves and thought you would be interested."

Oh.

Though Mr. Okamoto is new to the vice principal position, the former vice principal having retired in March, I have known him since I arrived in Kotoura. I knew him first as an employee overseeing business at the Board of Education and then was surprised to discover he was the proud father of one of my first English-speech contest participants.

Now as my school's vice principal, our connections are threefold. As a former social studies teacher, Mr. Okamoto has been generous in taking time to explain to me some of the finer points of Japanese culture. When I needed to know what kind of flowers were best for the jizo, he accompanied me to the supermarket, three-piece suit and all, to point out exactly which plants were appropriate. The fact that he remembered that the jizo needs a new offering cup to replace the cracked one is very touching.

"Thank you so much! I'd love to join you. When are you planning to go?"

"I'll be at your apartment in five minutes. We can drive together in my truck."

"Five minutes? Ah, yes, okay. See you soon." I stop myself from bowing into the unseeing phone and make a dive for my closet. Six minutes later (I did my best, okay?), I'm out the door, down the stairs, and climbing into the passenger seat of his small white pickup truck. We're zipping through the narrow back streets before I even have my seatbelt fully latched.

"I thought you probably wouldn't like to go to the funeral store by yourself," he observes, quite correctly. "This way I can explain the different items to you."

"You're absolutely right." I smile at him, noticing he's dressed down in sweat pants and a T-shirt. "Thank you for thinking of me. Is the store we're going to the—?"

"The one with the fifteen-foot gold Buddha out front?" he finishes. "Yes. I knew you'd be curious to go inside."

I bounce a bit on my seat in excitement. I can't help it. I've been driving past this tempting storefront for ages, dying to go inside. Well, not "dying" exactly. In fact, that's the problem. Just stopping by would be akin to visiting a funeral parlor to check out the viewing rooms. Not a great idea if you aren't in the market for a wake.

The door chimes gently as we enter, and Mr. Okamoto stops me almost immediately, drawing me over to a display full of cups. Gold, porcelain, engraved, painted—the selection is endless. I pick out a simple white one with a few lines of sutra running down one side. It's smooth, unpretentious, and looks like it will be easy to wash in the outdoor spigot I use. Happy with my selection, I turn to face the interior of the shop and draw in a breath.

It's gilded.

Gorgeously carved art fills every corner of the shop. I see lacquered wood, intricately shaped metal, and shiny onyx tables. I follow Mr. Okamoto to the incense aisle and am drawn in again by the variety. "They have coffee-scented incense?" I marvel.

"It's best to choose incense that would please your deceased relative," he tells me, pointing out the special "mother" blends and the decidedly manlier scents kept in dark brown boxes. "So if they loved coffee, why not welcome their soul home with the scent?" He turns to consult with one of the two shop workers who are hovering behind me. I wander over to the right to look at the selection of household shrines.

Most Japanese houses have a corner reserved for a shrine to the ancestors. The size and decoration vary according to circumstances, but they are always kept spotlessly clean, usually with fresh fruit and incense left out for a blessing. When I visit friends' houses, I am too shy to inspect them as closely as I would like. There's something intimidating about the framed pictures of their great-grandparents peering down from the walls.

Now though, I have no such qualms and lean closer to see the metalwork. Each shrine varies in price and style but has a common theme. Fierce, bearded dragons entwine with phoenix and lotus flowers around the border. Dark lacquered wood, enclosed in tall, pale cabinets, frames the displays, complete with small paper lanterns.

Mr. Okamoto comes over to join me. "Do you have any questions, Ellen Sensei?" He smiles at the two shop ladies. "She always asks the most unexpected things."

"Why are there dragons all over these?" I ask, pointing them out. "Isn't that kind of . . . aggressive?"

"Aggressive?" All three of them shake their heads. "The dragons and phoenix are for protection," one of the shop keepers explains. "They will guard and guide the dead."

"But . . . but in Christianity, the dragon is a symbol of the devil," I blurt out. "We would never put them on a gravestone."

"The devil? Really? No, no, no, thunderbolts perhaps, but a dragon is a pure guardian deity," they explain.

Vice Principal Okamoto studies me. "What images do you put on your Christian gravestones?"

"Lambs or doves," I answer.

"Lambs?" The shopkeeper smiles. "How in the world will a lamb protect you? They aren't very powerful."

"They're supposed to show peace," I venture. "As in, R.I.P? Rest in Peace?"

"It might be hard to rest peacefully if you only have a lamb to fight off the devil's thunderbolts," the shopkeeper says. "And surely a phoenix would be better than a dove."

"But a phoenix is a mythical . . ." I give up. Fawkes, the phoenix, did protect Harry Potter after all. Wait a sec, I might be overthinking this. We go to the register to pay for our purchases when one of the shop ladies hands me an extra package.

"Here's some incense for you," she says. "Thank you for coming in, it was very interesting to talk to you."

Vice Principal Okamoto beams at me. "How lucky! That's a generous gift."

I'm very thankful, but . . . "I'm sorry, but I don't have a grave to tend for Bon."

"You can use it for your house," they assure me. "Just be sure to lay down a dish to catch the ash." I bow my way out, and we leave.

Later that day I try burning a few sticks of incense but snuff them out quickly. It makes my apartment smell like a graveyard.

Maybe I should have asked for the coffee-scented kind.

20

In the Arms of a Faith Community

Jane

*Lamb of God, who takes away the sins of the world, have
mercy on us.
Lamb of God, who takes away the sins of the world, have
mercy on us.
Lamb of God, who takes away the sins of the world, grant us peace.*
—from the Roman Catholic Mass and
the Lutheran Book of Worship

My year of teaching eighth graders has been one of the best working experiences of my career as a math teacher. These students are smart, hardworking, and they make me laugh. What more could a teacher wish for? Yet they are also normal fourteen-year-olds, which comes with sulking, prevaricating, and well-concealed bullying. And so amid the many successes, I feel a continual need for prayer.

Their homeroom teacher, on the other hand, has had a terrible year. Not because of the students, though. Early in the year, her husband was diagnosed with cancer, and they have spent much of the last few months travelling back and forth to the University of Michigan Medical Center in Ann Arbor. Mrs. Matyas is a longtime friend. Much of my prayer time and many candles have been offered up for her and her husband.

But despite our prayers and the best that medical science has to offer, he passes away.

Our students are troubled and uncertain about what to do for a teacher whom they truly love. For some of them, this is the first time they have personally known a bereaved person. This is a Catholic school, and even though not all the students are Catholic, the community guides them through the rituals of visitation, funeral, prayers, and expressions of sympathy. They are instructed to wear collared shirts and ties, dresses and hard shoes, and to bring rosary beads with them to the funeral home. A collection is taken up for flowers. Classes are cancelled for the funeral.

After the long days of ritual and mourning, the students are back at their desks with their geometry books open in front of them. I am beginning the lesson when the principal comes over the public address system announcing: "LOCKDOWN: intruder in the building."

I knew this was coming; we teachers had been warned of the drill, but the students are taken off guard. Their eyes lock on mine, and I reassure them by remaining completely calm. "You know where to go," I tell them.

They stand and move quickly into the computer room next to ours which, unlike my classroom, has no windows. We crowd into a corner that has cement block walls and is not directly in line with either door. I throw the locks, and two students help me tape black paper over the small panes of glass in each door. The students upend a table, and we crouch on the floor behind it in absolute silence. Unlike the casual routine of a tornado drill, they are visibly tense until after the "all clear" announcement is made by the principal. I think about the severe restrictions on gun and knife ownership in Japan. At least Ellen doesn't have to do these awful drills with her students.

It's creepy. It's necessary. It's also a depressing thing to do at the end of an already depressing week.

When we are back in civilized positions at our desks, and I have redirected the students to thinking about obtuse angles and protractors, Kristen raises her hand and says, "Mrs. Knuth, can we ask you something?"

I look up at the serious sound of her voice. "Absolutely."

"Some of us have been talking, and we're wondering what we can do to help Mrs. Matyas. We feel bad about her husband, but we don't know what to say or do."

I am touched. "You are doing real well. You were all at the funeral or the visitation. I'm sure you've been praying for her?"

Sierra exchanges glances with Kristen. "But when she comes back to school, what do we do then?"

"Ah, I see what you mean." I look at their ten sincere faces for a long minute, thinking. "The only thing a teacher really needs from her students is for them to be nice to each other. Maybe you never knew that? For us teachers, the worst days are the ones where students pick on classmates or are exclusive and cliquish. If you do your best to be nice to each other for the next few weeks, you will make her job so easy she won't have to worry about teaching at all."

They all look at me doubtfully.

"Seriously?" Samantha asks. "Just being nice to each other will help *her?*"

"Yep."

"Well, then. That's what we'll do." She looks at each of her classmates in turn, and they all nod.

21

The Difference of One Vowel

Ellen

It's the Friday after graduation, and a sense of relief fills the staff room. Once again, we have managed to get all the fifteen-year-olds safely graduated and enrolled in various high schools. Compulsory schooling ends after junior high in Japan, so we never have a guarantee that all the graduates will continue on to higher education. Luckily, this year everyone has passed the stringent entrance exams and has been accepted to a preparatory or technical school. Each teen will now start forging his or her own path toward whatever dream is worth chasing.

We can breathe.

Though I teach all the students in the school, my desk is in the third-year teachers' aisle. Thus I am officially a member of the third-year teaching squad. In celebration of a successful year, the seven of us are departing on a three-day trip to Nagasaki early tomorrow morning. I've never been to the southern tip of the main Japanese island, and I'm excited to see the old trading colony Dejima and visit the small house that St. Francis Xavier lived in during his missionary days.

I've also made a special request to visit the ruins of Urakami Cathedral. Though well-known in Japan, many foreigners are unaware that the atomic bomb dropped on Nagasaki exploded directly over the

Catholic cathedral, destroying everything in the surrounding area but leaving behind scorched saint statues and arches. It's the A-bomb memorial of Nagasaki, a silent testimony to everything that's lost in war.

I glance at the clock. There is a little more than an hour before I can go home and pack for the trip. It's the beginning of March, so Tottori is still chilly, but Nagasaki promises to be showing the first signs of spring. I'll have to dig out my spring jacket from storage. My mind is completely occupied with packing details when it happens.

A strange buzzing fills the room. It's a vibrating, pulsing sound from every desk, and it takes me a second to realize what's happening.

Every cell phone in the school has lit up simultaneously.

The probability of everyone getting a call or text at the exact same time is so miniscule, it's impossible. I grab my phone. A screen I've never seen before is displayed. It's an earthquake warning, not for anywhere close. In fact it's a warning for the northern area, hundreds and hundreds of miles away, but looking at the warning, even I, an earthquake novice, can tell this is big.

All the teachers in the room start to grab their phones. There's no panic—in fact no one says much, but the gym teacher gets up to turn on the TV in the break corner. As the whispers start, I open Facebook. Friends who live farther north are panicking: "Did you FEEL that?" reads a status. "Evacuating to the school roof," states another. "I'm okay, but we've got a tsunami warning." I type a brief message to the effect that we're all tuning into the disaster, and stand up to see the TV.

The news is showing a live feed from Sendai in Miyagi Prefecture. I visited there a few years back on a spontaneous February vacation with my host sister Kana. It's a beautiful area, all majestic mountains and pine forests. I remember flying into the airport and taking the speedy airport shuttle train to the city center to start our weekend.

Now the TV is showing something incomprehensible. A dark black wave of water is swallowing the land. The terminals of the airport that I used are disappearing under debris. The helicopter footage shows people scrambling onto roofs, fighting for handholds above the surging sea. The station switches cameras to a wide view of the wave rolling over farmland. We watch horrified as cars drive parallel to the approaching disaster, unaware of or unable to escape the wave.

The teacher next to me, a burly man who is famous for not saying more than needs to be said, starts to plead with the drivers on the screen. "Run! No! Don't turn that way! My God . . ." He falls silent as car after car disappears from view. The camera feed cuts out.

We're all frozen. Tohaku JHS is less than a mile from the Japanese sea. This wave is on the opposite ocean—but should we be evacuating? The small map of Japan superimposed on the lower corner of the screen is flashing red. Not just the northern area now, but the whole of the eastern coast. Now Hokkaido. The southern islands. Nagasaki. Strangely, only Tottori and our neighboring prefecture are yellow. We're in a pocket on the coast which, though still not a comforting green color, is only yellow.

Yellow is fine. I'll take yellow.

The head math teacher of my squad walks in. "What's going on?" he asks, and we remember that his college-age daughter lives in Sendai. There's a suffocating moment of urgency, and then everyone moves. People grab phones, open computers, run to the office, go check on the students. Unsure of what to do, I keep watching the TV. The reporters are all wearing helmets. The news headquarters, based in Tokyo, is experiencing aftershocks so frequent it starts to seem strange when the camera shows a steady feed.

I walk blindly back to my desk. Students, with their unerring ability to tell when the adults aren't telling them something, are loitering in the doors. Teachers shoo them out, order them to start the end-of-week class meetings. The principal calls an emergency meeting.

The math teacher can't reach his daughter.

Facebook is still open on my computer. My newsfeed is exploding. As phones start to fail, people are turning to the site to reach friends and relatives. "Can someone call my mom?" reads one. "I'm fine, but I can't stay at the computer." "Hiro, call me!" pleads another. "Is grandma okay? Mom can't get through."

Someone has made the decision to let today's club activities continue as usual. The chance of the tsunami reaching us is slim. "Shouldn't we tell the students?" I ask my coworker and friend, Kira Sensei.

She purses her lips and shakes her head. "They'll hear from their parents," she says. "It's better to let them play sports right now." It's not much, but two more hours of ignorance is all we can give them.

What seems like an age later, I'm gathering my things to go home. "We'll pick you up at five tomorrow morning," Kira Sensei says. "Okay?"

I stare at her blankly.

"For the Nagasaki trip?" she prods.

It doesn't occur to me to question the wisdom of moving from our safe yellow zone to a city decidedly outlined in red. I nod and apologize for leaving early, per usual. But today, other teachers have already gone home, a rarity in this workaholic school.

I walk up the five flights of stairs to my apartment instead of taking the elevator, noting with relief that, though a bit older, this building is made of concrete. Not wood. My apartment seems dark. I turn on all the lights.

My reliable Japanese cell phone is suspiciously silent. Instead of the normal four bars, I have next-to-no signal. But my apartment's Internet connection is still functioning. In the twenty minutes since I last logged in, every friend I have in Southeast Asia and Australia seems to have written on my wall or sent me a message. I'm surprised. Surely at least some of them know that Tottori is nowhere near the quake. Then I remember.

My residence is listed as Tohaku County. The tsunami is currently destroying Tohoku.

What, in real life, the difference of hundreds of miles is—to my friends, the difference of a vowel. And the panic induced by these images is enough to make anyone forget to double-check the spelling.

I write a new, firmer status reinforcing my safety and asking for prayers for the north. I also plug in my TV and turn it on for the first time in a year. There seems to be budding trouble in Fukushima, another beautiful area I passed through on a trip farther north. The only reason I know the Japanese word for "nuclear" is because I studied it in preparation for visiting the Nagasaki bomb site. It's strange how quickly that vocabulary became normal.

I'm watching my computer clock. It's still early morning in Michigan, but I am absolutely determined to be the first bearer of bad news. From years of saying the rosary together every morning, I know that my parents are awakened daily by their clock radio that switches on to NPR's early morning news broadcast. I know what the top headline is going to be, and I also know that it's absolutely essential that I spare them the panic and fear of hearing this without knowing if I'm okay.

My clock informs me that it's only 5:15 a.m. in Michigan. The reporters on TV are hiding under their broadcast desk as a light fixture sways above them. Outside my apartment, the sun is setting. I thought it set ages ago.

I open Skype and call.

22

Five-Fifteen A.M.

Jane

The phone rings next to the bed and I answer it on the second ring without turning on the light. Ellen's voice in my ear says, "I'm sorry to wake you up. I just want you to know that I'm fine."

"Hi, Ellie," I mumble, and squint at the glowing numbers on the clock radio. *5:15*. "What do you mean '*you're fine*'—why are you fine?"

"There was an earthquake, but it was on the other side of the country—it was a big one."

"Oh, no! Are many people hurt?" I'm fully awake now.

Dean, who has been listening, sits up and motions to me to put the phone on speaker. He clicks on the bedside light.

Ellen describes the midday catastrophe, the tsunami reports, the worries about the nuclear plants, and the dreadful videos on the news stations. The words catch in her throat, and she stops speaking.

While I try to comfort her, Dean heads down to the living room to switch on his computer and I follow him, still listening to Ellen's descriptions of the confusion and the distress all around the country.

The conversation moves back and forth with questions that don't have answers and fears that don't have hiding places. Eventually, there isn't anything more we can say to each other because there is so much unknown. Ellen is exhausted and needs to make phone calls to her friends in other countries. Would we be able to call her grandmother and the other relatives? We promise her our prayers and arrange to talk next in her morning, our evening.

Within minutes of hanging up the phone, I don't have an accurate recollection of this conversation. Did she say anything about after-shocks? Has the American consulate put out a bulletin? Should we be attempting to arrange an evacuation for our daughter?

Dean and I, in our pajamas, are watching the computer screen, chasing the various reports from news services worldwide. The videos of the rushing sea are horrific. We gasp and hold our heads in disbelief. Dean wakes up Martha, and she opens up her computer to scan mul-tiple news sources simultaneously.

This early-morning tumult goes on for the entire day. I make a dozen phone calls to reassure relatives that we have been in contact with Ellen. I repeat what she told us over and over, offering reassurance but no precise answers. My mind is in Japan. I can concentrate on very few of my other duties or tasks, so I watch the news feeds between cups of tea and phone calls. Dean calls me from work at noon and says, "I've been watching the reports on the Fukushima nuclear plant. Have you seen them?"

"The American channels are making a bigger fuss over it than the Japanese news services," I point out. "But there's always hype from our media before anything is really clear. And the Japanese are known for downplaying every crisis, so I'm not sure what to think."

"That's why I'm following the Australian sources. It doesn't sound good. The State Department hasn't issued an evacuation order yet, but some other countries are starting to advise their people to leave. I'm looking into ways to get her out of the country and checking with all the commercial airlines."

"We have our tickets for the end of the month. Would it be possible to switch those over for her use?"

"That's three weeks away. It might be too late by then."

I am silent.

Dean says, "We'll talk to her tonight. By then, she will know more about how it looks on the ground."

"It's her second language," I wonder aloud. "How will she be able to sort out truth from PR?"

"She'll know more than we can find out here, that's for sure. We'll have to trust her judgment, Jane."

"*She's only twenty-five!*" Even I can hear the wail in my voice.

23

Coming Down

Ellen

Four hundred miles is a long way to drive. When we third-year teachers planned our end-of-the-year trip to Nagasaki, we allotted nine hours for the journey, assuming Saturday traffic and road conditions might add to the travel time. As it is, we've completed the entire distance in seven. There is no one on the roads, no one in the restaurants, only a handful of people in the convenience store we stop at to buy canned coffee.

The one place we encounter a group of people is in front of the rest-stop television. The TV, usually tuned to the weather channel and traffic reports, shows a news loop of buildings crumbling under the force of the wave. Bricks and masonry barely miss fleeing pedestrians as they scramble out of buildings in Tokyo. The ticker running at the bottom of the screen reports the strength of each aftershock as they hit.

Kira Sensei and I stand next to each other, watching in silence. Kira Sensei, a beautiful science teacher whose firm but friendly teaching style is one I try to emulate, is originally from Kobe. I wonder if this coverage brings back unpleasant memories of the Great Hanshin earthquake of 1995, but I don't ask. The heat from my coffee can burns my fingers, and I take a sip. It's too sweet, and I realize I've absentmindedly purchased my least favorite brand. Before I can decide whether to buy another, we move away from the building and back to the car.

We unanimously vote to watch *The Karate Kid* remake instead of NHK news on the car's TV. Halfway through a discussion about whether Jayden Smith would actually be allowed to wear cornrow braids at a Chinese private school, my phone buzzes. I'm surprised, first because service has been spotty all day, second because the number is Tohaku JHS. Why they would call me out of an entire car full of teachers with seniority, I have no idea. I answer.

"Ellen Sensei, this is Principal Ishiga. We've had a call from your prefectural supervisor Akiyama-san. She's trying to locate you."

Mayumi Akiyama is in charge of all the JETs in Tottori Prefecture, but aside from the occasional conference or e-mail exchange, we have had little contact. Before I can voice my surprise, my call-waiting tone sounds in my ear. "Thank you, Principal Ishiga, I think she's calling me now. Excuse me." I switch lines. "Hello?"

"Hello, is this Ellen? This is Mayumi Akiyama with the Tottori Prefectural Board of Education." Mayumi's usually energetic voice is still cheerful but undeniably stressed.

"Hi, Mayumi, yes, it's me." The other teachers in the car have turned down the volume on the movie to make it easier for me to talk and to give them a chance to catch the meaning of my English words. "What's up?"

"Oh, good! I'm glad I finally reached you. We have to locate all foreign nationals and verify their safety—you're the last one. Are you really on a trip to Nagasaki?"

"Er . . . yes. We had planned it and decided not to cancel." I've been excited about this trip for weeks, but now I'm not so sure. "Is that okay? Do you need me to come back?"

"No, no, no, but I needed to locate you so I can complete the list. You're with Japanese teachers, right? And they're aware that Nagasaki is still under a wave warning?"

"Yes, we saw it on the news."

"Good. Just be careful, and keep an eye on your phone for alerts." Mayumi ends the conversation as abruptly as it began. "Have a safe trip."

My car mates look at me curiously as I hang up the phone. Kira Sensei, who has a good grasp of English, leans back slightly to talk to me. "Your supervisor? She's calling?"

"Yes, they are making a list of foreigners," I say, not sure if I want to talk about this. "A list of all the foreign teachers so they know we're safe."

"To give to your government probably," the social studies teacher remarks. "Have you heard France is offering to evacuate French citizens in the areas around Fukushima? Apparently, they have a plane waiting in Tokyo."

"Why would they leave the country completely?" someone asks, but no one answers. The next question is directed to the head math teacher sitting in the front passenger seat. "Hamahashi Sensei, have you heard from your daughter?"

"Not yet," he says, and we all turn back to *The Karate Kid*. That Jayden Smith sure has some good kicks.

Nagasaki is a pretty city on the bay, a jumbled mixture of architectural styles and precisely paved streets. We park the car in a public lot and set off down the main tourist street lined with shops and restaurants with signs beseeching us to try their wares. The itinerary for today allotted more time for driving than we ultimately needed, so now we have a few extra hours for souvenir shopping.

By the time we stop for ice cream, I'm already holding two bags. I wait outside, opting to forgo the traditional sweet potato-flavored treat that's advertised.

As I scan the street around me, a sign catches my eye: *National Treasure Oura Catholic Church of the 26 Martyrs*. A red arrow kindly informs me to proceed further down the street another 800 meters.

Seeing that the line for sweet potato ice cream is moving slowly, I step in to tell Kira Sensei where I'm going and set off on my own. The street narrows and takes on a sharp incline, and I'm panting by the time I reach the bottom of the staircase.

As with most Japanese places of worship, this church has been built on top of a hill. There are four steep flights of stairs between me and the gleaming white structure, but the steeple beckons and I sling my souvenir bags over my shoulder with determination. Plaques along the way inform me the church was built in 1853. This was soon after the reformist government abolished the seclusion policy—which had closed off Japan from the outside world for two hundred years—instituted by the shoguns (warlord rulers), and Christians who had been practicing their religion in secret came out of hiding. I imagine it must have taken some courage, even in the new political climate, to erect a structure in memory of the priests and citizens crucified by the samurai so soon after their rule had been toppled.

I near the end of the climb, and at the top of the stairs, as if she's been waiting for me, is a statue of the Virgin Mary. Her eyes are cast heavenward and her hands are clasped under her chin, but I can't tell if it's in prayer or grief. Japanese tourists around me stop to take pictures, but I move toward the building.

It doesn't seem to be a functioning church anymore, though the pews, kneelers, and holy water fonts are still there. Barriers have been erected between the altar and the rest of the church, probably to discourage overenthusiastic selfies. But the gorgeous soaring ceiling and softly tinted stained glass still invoke an air of worship, and I plop down on one of the pews at the back, letting my bags fall next to me on the floor. The kneelers look very old, not a hint of padding, so I decide to stay seated.

For several minutes I stare at the altar. I want to pray. I really do. But there are no words. Not an informal conversation. Not even a plea. I honestly have no idea what to even think. So I just stare at the windows, look at the carvings and the statues.

My head is full of screen captures from all the news reports I've seen on TV today. My thoughts are completely submerged beneath this wave, and there's no way to surface. I finally give up and let the images play. I'm stunned. Maybe I should cry. But all I can really do is sit here and stare at these windows.

I think God probably understands this type of prayer the best.

Finally, I stand, take a picture of the interior on my cell phone, and leave. It's easier going down the stairs than up, and I'm nearly at the bottom when I meet Kira Sensei coming to fetch me.

"We're moving on," she announces. "Hamahashi Sensei got a call from his wife; their daughter is okay. Shall we go have a beer?"

"Yes, beer sounds great." We walk back to the group together, away from the church on the hill. I don't look back.

24

Folding Cranes

Jane

Martha is folding cranes. She is folding them in her bedroom, at her desk. The origami birds are multicolored and flowered, gold-tinged and sparkly. The sizes vary according to the size of the paper. Some are as tiny as a bumblebee, but the average one fits nicely in the palm of my hand. She has been doing this for three days. It is too depressing to watch the news any longer, so I wander into her room and look over her shoulder.

"They're beautiful," I tell her.

"It's a symbol of hope," she says without looking up, "especially for nuclear disasters." She doesn't have to explain more because we both know the story of the Thousand Cranes. I read it to her and Ellen when they were young.

"How many do you have?" I ask.

"I'm not sure," she answers, "but I'm going to try to make a thousand."

I nod, and watch her fold, crease, and rotate the paper. She seems so calm. "Can I ask you something?" I say as I sit down on her bed.

"Sure."

"When you and Ellen were growing up, there were several tragic disasters: Oklahoma City when you were in grade school, then Columbine in junior high, and 9/11 followed by the wars in Afghanistan and Iraq during your high school years. I wondered at the time how your generation was affected. The news coverage was so prolonged and intense, and the entire country went into mourning—it's all we talked about. I knew these awful things would make a mark on young people, but I wasn't sure how."

"Of course, they affected us." She keeps folding.

"Yeah, so . . . in what way?"

"I don't understand what you're asking."

I stop. What am I asking? "Well, it's like this: I had a more protected childhood. Bad things happened, but the news wasn't broadcasting it twenty-four hours a day. There was no Internet to check everything everywhere in the world. It all seemed much farther away—in other countries where none of us would ever visit. When Oklahoma City happened, I looked at the photos of the children being taken out of the childcare facility and I thought, 'That could have been my child.' When 9/11 happened, it felt like that could have been my husband's workplace. When Columbine happened—you girls were students, it could have been your school. These things hit so hard because it feels like it could have been here, it could have been us."

Martha shakes her head. "I don't think that way at all."

"You don't? What goes through your head when you see a disaster like this tsunami?"

She finishes a pink crane and adds it to the pile. "I think to myself, *It wasn't me this time. Keep going.*" She looks at me with sympathetic eyes. "I'll bet that's what Ellen is thinking, too."

We sit for several minutes in silence while Martha continues to fold cranes.

Then I say, "You know what Ellen told me about why she decided to stay? Even though many of her friends are leaving the country, she is hanging on because of one of her students. When the schools reopened and Ellen went back to the grade school, a little first grader saw her in the hallway and came running up and hugged her around the knees. She said, 'Ellen Sensei, Ellen Sensei, you're still here!' Ellen asked, 'Where else would I be?'"

"The little one told her, 'My parents said you might go home, that maybe you wouldn't teach us anymore!' So that was the moment when Ellen decided she really had to stay."

Martha nods. "I get that. It's essential to kids that the adults aren't afraid." She finishes another crane, adds it to the pile on her desk, and reaches for more paper.

I ask, "Do you need some help?"

She tells me that her three cousins are coming that evening to help. I mention that the Catholic school where I taught math the previous year had called that morning and asked about Ellen—one of dozens of similar calls. "I'll bet the students could make these," I say, picking one up and looking it over. "If someone taught them, that is."

Martha stops working and riffles the stack of unfolded squares of paper with her thumb. She chews the inside of her cheek for a moment, thinking it over. "Can you ask a teacher or two to let me into their classroom for an hour?"

"Which age groups?"

She closes one eye. "No younger than third grade, I think."

25

The Caring Network
Luncheon

Jane

One thing they don't tell you up front in the publishing business is that a large part of an author's job is to give speeches to groups of people who are eating lunch.

It is the day before Dean and I will fly to Japan, exactly three weeks since the earthquake and tsunami. I am dressed in shiny pumps and a pink sweater, standing at a microphone, looking at the annual gathering of the Caring Network. This group of 150 people is at the forefront of the struggle to prevent abortions in our town, and this luncheon is one of their fund-raisers.

Our thrift store helps poor people, and we know firsthand that poor women are the ones most under pressure to terminate their pregnancies. We assist pregnant women who can't pay their bills or feed their children, so I guess one might argue that we prevent abortions on the side. But that's not why I've been given the microphone. I am under no illusions about why I was chosen as the speaker for this gathering. A fund-raising lunch succeeds better if someone stands up and tells good stories to the donors—simple as that. I've eaten incredible quantities of tasty chicken breasts and asparagus this spring.

My problem is that I have not been thinking about pregnant women much recently. My thoughts, fears, and prayers are all in Japan. When I wrote the speech, the first stories that came to me were not very hopeful. But Martha's cranes have been multiplying steadily for three weeks, and now, they are hanging in long streamers all over my house. At the last minute, the speech came together based on those beautifully folded bits of paper.

Fran, the director of Catholic Family Services, introduces me and I begin:

"Thank you, Laurie, and Fran, and Susan. I am truly honored to be here today. When Susan called me and asked me to come, she told me to tell Stories of Hope, the theme for today.

"Well, since that's the only kind of story I know how to tell, I thought: this will be easy.

"First Story: My daughter Ellen lives and works in Japan."

I pause because a gasp and murmur goes round the room. Startled, I look out at the audience and wave my hand reassuringly.

"No need to worry—she's fine. She lives on the southwest coast, far away from the multiple disasters. But she's understandably nervous and out of sorts, and she asked me to gather prayers for the people of Japan. Some of my daughter's Japanese friends contacted her and asked her to pray for their country. They are Buddhists, and they said to her: 'We know you and your family are prayerful people, so we thought of asking you to help us in this way.' I was so grateful to be able to tell her about all the people I would be able to pass that request to this month.

"I told Ellen, 'I'll be speaking to fourteen different groups in the next few weeks; I think that's going to work out just fine.' My husband, Dean, and I are leaving to visit Ellen tomorrow. So you can pray a little bit for us too.

"Meanwhile, my other daughter, Martha, must have felt a little out of sorts, too, with her entire family going to Japan, so she started to fold origami cranes. These little paper birds are a symbol of hope in Japan, especially for children. People fold and string the cranes and hang them at the shrines, as signs of hope."

I hold up one of Martha's cranes for the audience to see.

"When word got out about Martha folding cranes, other children joined in. Her cousins came over to our house and started folding, then her friends. St. Monica School called to ask how Ellen was doing, and I let slip about Martha's project, and so cranes were folded by the students at St. Monica, St. Augustine, the youth group at St. Ambrose, Martha's friends, her cousins, and members of the Western Michigan University Japanese Club.

"It became an impromptu network, everyone folding cranes out of hope for the safety of others . . . kind of like Caring Network . . .

"I brought some of them along today to show you what hope looks like when it is fashioned by the nimble fingers of earnest, prayerful children."

Here, I bend down to the large satchel at my feet and lift four long strings of origami cranes, holding them up so they stretch from above my head to the floor. The audience takes in a long and sudden breath, and applause unexpectedly flows through the room. I drape the cranes over the top of the lectern and resume speaking:

"Second Story:

"What is our hope? Our greatest hope? I'll let you ponder that a second or two.

"For me, the one great hope I have is that all those stories in the Bible are true. Especially that one about the Resurrection.

"Other than the Resurrection—the one I really, really want to be true is the story in Luke's Gospel about Mary. The story where she is young and pregnant and unmarried, and God convinces Joseph to take care of her anyway, and then God sends angels to celebrate the birth of the baby Jesus, and then God sends poor people to celebrate, then he sends wise men to bring gifts. And what started out looking like a scandal instead looks like a miracle.

"And then it all gets messy again. The king turns crazy and starts killing babies, but God sends angels again and Joseph cashes in the wise men's gifts and helps Mary and Jesus to escape. Whew!

"Great story. I really want that one to be true.

"When my sister was in college, she had a friend her senior year who was a very nice girl but not a churchgoing girl at all. They were both theater majors . . . lots of late nights, especially on weekends . . . so not a lot of early Sundays going on there.

"One day, her roommate told her the story about how when she was a freshman and she became pregnant, her boyfriend suddenly wasn't her boyfriend anymore.

"She took her broken heart home to her parents, and suddenly, she wasn't their daughter anymore.

"She came back to Kalamazoo with no money and no emotional support. She felt that her only choice was to have an abortion. But if you only have one choice, then you don't really have a choice at all. To have a choice there must be at least two alternatives, right?

"A friend told her to call Catholic Family Services. Now this was years ago, before Caring Network and its apartments and mother-friends and parenting classes and all the other choices you folks offer. But Catholic Family Services found a family in town who took this girl into their home and provided for her during her pregnancy. She gave the baby up for adoption and went back to school and when my sister knew her, she was a senior, ready to graduate.

"And all that time she was putting herself through school, she was so grateful for the choice you had given her.

"This is a true story. And it sounds an awful lot like that old story in Luke's Gospel.

"Many of you good people in this room today have played the part of Joseph. You have been the protectors of the young pregnant girls who are afraid and without choices.

"Many of you have played the part of the poor people and the angels, rejoicing at the birth of the babies.

"Many of you have played the part of the wise men, providing the lavish gifts needed to sustain the young families in those early struggles.

"My one great hope is that all those stories in the Bible are true.

"Thank you for showing me that one of my favorite stories was not only true back then, but it's still true today.

"And thank you for inviting me here today."

26

Over the Top of the World

Jane

The shortest route from Michigan to Japan takes us over the top of the world. Our plane departs from Detroit Metro Airport and heads northwest. We chase the sun, nearly keeping pace with its traverse toward the horizon. Out of the tiny window, I look down on the southern Alaskan coast, and after that, the ice floes in the Arctic Ocean.

This bothers me. I am oriented to travel east and west, maybe south, but never farther north than Ontario, Canada. I question Dean, but he assures me that we will not venture over Russian airspace, but from here on the top of the world, we will follow the north Pacific islands all the way south to Japan.

After nearly thirteen hours, we begin to descend, and I can make out the outlines of the northern province of Hokkaido, near where Rodger lived and taught. I think of him and his family and say some prayers. I feel a conflicted comfort to know that Rodger wasn't caught in the horror of the earthquake and tsunami.

We are approaching the earth's surface with the lower hum of the engines and soon, other passengers are pointing out the windows and exclaiming over the sight of the devastated coastline. I don't know what the cities below me used to look like, but it is not difficult to make out the ragged line of unrecognizable jumble that cuts between what remains of every town and the sea. From our height, it resembles the high-tide line of seaweed, driftwood, and shells left on beaches throughout the world, but I know that this flotsam is made up of crushed and shattered buildings, vehicles, and boats.

And their occupants. Four thousand people are still listed as missing, with another sixteen thousand confirmed dead.

I can't stop myself from looking down.

27

The Sakura Are Late This Year

Jane

Sakura is the Japanese word for the extraordinarily beautiful cherry trees that blossom throughout this island country every year. The cherry trees in Washington, D.C., are offspring of the trees I am gazing at now, a gift from the people of Japan in 1912. The trees in Kotoura are not yet in full bloom, their buds tightly knotted against the unseasonably cold temperatures. This southwest community is visibly untouched by the multiple disasters. There are no power outages like we experienced on our arrival in Tokyo; the food supply is uninterrupted because much of Japan's food comes from this rural province; the water is uncontaminated. The people are subdued, as is our daughter, but they are going about their usual lives.

"**Ganbatte**," they encourage each other over and over: *Do your best.*

Ellen's friend, Junko, an ardent hostess, insists on us staying in her home with her husband and three young children. They give us the children's bedroom, which, at first glance, is a large space furnished only with straw **tatami** mats and a few toys. Junko walks across the open floor and pulls on a closet door. Inside we see large, rolled-up futon mattresses, folded sheets, and pillows. She spreads these out on the tatami mats and tucks all the linens neatly around the bulky cushions. She hands us towels and shows us where to find both the toilet room and the shower room, located separately from each other.

When Junko leaves us for a moment, Ellen quickly explains the importance of changing into special slippers when we use the toilet room. "Don't walk in there in your stocking feet, and never wear the toilet slippers in other parts of the house—don't forget or it will be very embarrassing."

Dean looks from the dainty Japanese toilet slippers down to his size twelve feet, and raises an eyebrow at her.

"You're just going to have to make it work, Pa."

The next day is Sunday, and because there are no Christian churches, and since Junko personifies Japanese hospitality, she has arranged to take us to the neighborhood Shinto shrine.

"I am so very sorry," she says in English. "The sakura are late this year. I hope you are not very disappointed? Please excuse this problem."

We do not understand why she is apologizing for the trees, but we assure her that we are not in the least unhappy. Ellen explains that, despite the hibernating sakura, it is, nevertheless, time for the spring festival, and everyone in the neighborhood will be at the shrine to celebrate. Traditionally, the sakura festivals are joyful holidays characterized by outdoor gatherings, music, and generously flowing sake. All throughout the country, the recent multiple national disasters have cast somberness over the planned events, and the citizens are unsure of how, and how much, to party.

And on top of everything else—an undeserved misfortune—the trees have refused to bloom.

At the neighborhood shrine, we walk the garden-like grounds, and Ellen introduces us to nearly every person we pass. Each of them feels it is necessary to apologize for their recalcitrant trees. Her students, their parents, her neighbors, and even the local business owners all bow in welcome and then say, "**Sumimasen** (I'm sorry). The sakura are late this year."

We, in turn, bow and offer condolences for the devastation to their country. They nod seriously and point out the other trees and bushes that are blooming, hoping that this is compensation. Ellen moves us along toward the row of booths set up around the shrine. The proprietors are hawking fried squid on sticks, red bean pastries, and cotton candy. There are tables filled with rummage-sale items and souvenirs, and every family has spread out a blanket on the ground under the sakura trees. It appears they are camping for the day, hoping their patient presence will compel the flower buds to open. Shiba Inus, a breed of dog native to Japan, wave their curved tails, and doubled-over grandmothers spoon steaming noodles into bowls. Teenagers offer us donut holes with tiny octopus arms reaching through the golden crust. I eat these in a single bite to avoid seeing what is inside.

Outside the front of a gray wooden building, black-haired children carrying goldfish in bulging, water-filled plastic bags wait in line to have their photos taken with the Shinto priest. He is dressed in traditional robes and laughs easily as he lifts the youngsters in his arms and talks with their parents. To me, it looks something like the weekly scene outside Catholic churches where the priest in his vestments greets the parishioners as they leave the sanctuary.

At the steps to the shrine, imitating the people in front of us, we light incense sticks and wave them over our arthritic joints. After that, we ritually wash our hands in the flowing fountain and clap them together softly in front of a statue of a fox. Inside the building, Ellen shows us how to toss coins into the wooden slats near the doorway, don communal slippers, and kneel respectfully on the cold wooden floor in front of what appears to be a large cymbal. After a few moments, we stand up, slip our feet back into our shoes, and head outside to the food booths to buy lunch. Although this is not Mass, it is Sunday and I find comfort in small rituals and putting respect for the spiritual above filling physical needs.

"Why are there so few people inside the shrine?" I ask Ellen as we walk down the steps. "Did we miss the ceremony?"

"A shrine isn't a church, Ma," she explains. "They don't gather here in a congregation. On a festival day like this one, everyone will come in family groups, make their offerings, show their respect for the dead, then leave the building for the next people to visit. On occasion, someone will stay a long time. I've listened to some lovely chants, but it's not meant for communal participation."

"Well then, what is the priest's job?"

"Unless it's a major shrine in a big pilgrimage site, the priest isn't a full-time employee. He and his family take care of the buildings and perform the coming-of-age rituals, funerals, and celebrate holidays like this one, but he works a regular job during the week. In most cases, the priest inherits his vocation from his father or grandfather, and he probably has no choice in the matter."

Dean is staring at the wood carving alongside the main door of the building and pulls out his camera to snap several shots from different angles. "Ellen," he says. "Could you ask one of your friends what story is depicted in this panel?"

We gaze up at the gray wooden relief that frames one side of the double door. In this scene, there's a lot of action going on. A fierce samurai, outfitted with armor, a quiver of arrows, and a cutlass, is dashing headlong toward us. Swords, spears, and arrows fly in all directions, but he appears to be unscathed. His face is scrunched up with either fear or anger. Tucked in the crook of the samurai's left arm is a baby, sleeping peacefully amid the tumult. It is not your usual battle scene.

Ellen asks her neighbors about the story on the panel, but with embarrassed apologies and bows, the locals admit that they believe the carving must be very ancient, and the tale perhaps forgotten. One of the neighbors tells her to wait a moment, and he will find out what the priest knows.

He comes back, and we learn that this samurai is one of the legendary fighters of the warring period, pledged to protect the royal family. At that time in history, there was a recently widowed empress who gave birth to a baby boy. The competitors for the throne in Kyoto were determined to murder the little prince, so the samurai escaped with the baby to the remote and mountainous region of Tottori to protect him from assassins. They kept him hidden in the very town where we are standing until he came of age and could claim his birthright.

Listening to Ellen translate the story, I am struck by the similarity to the biblical account of the massacre of the innocents in Bethlehem shortly after Jesus' birth. "It's like the story of the flight to Egypt," I remark.

"Hmm . . . yeah. I guess it is a little," Ellen says. "But this one is history, not religion."

I start to point out that Jesus' birth is historical, too, but she has already turned to thank her friends. They are engrossed in discussing the ancient account of the empress's son amongst themselves, counting centuries on their fingers and arguing about dynastic lineages. Dean's question has taken them away from the failed blossoms and the tragedy engulfing their country, and into their shared history and beliefs.

Ellen's statement is making me wonder if we need a discussion like this too. But I sense now is not the time. Perhaps it's time for another one of those listening gifts.

The next morning, Dean and I are on our own. It is the first day of classes for the new school year. Ellen has many duties, but she has arranged that we will visit the school for the opening ceremony in the gymnasium later in the afternoon.

For the first part of the day, Dean and I decide to take a scenic walk along the shoreline. It is only a few blocks from Ellen's apartment, so we wrap ourselves in jackets and wind our way through the neighborhood. Grandmothers bow to us when we pass them on the sidewalks, and so do the teenagers.

Many homes line the coast, just as we would expect to find in any American city, but to our surprise, the residences face the internal streets, not the sea. In fact, they have few windows looking toward the ocean at all. As we walk the narrow seaside pavement with one side bordered by a twenty-foot tsunami wall and locking gates, and the other by garages, trash cans, and kitchen gardens, we realize that this is not prime real estate. There are no docks with pleasure boats, no sundecks, no private beaches. The beaches are piled high with broken concrete and wired-together barriers to keep the untrustworthy water at bay. The only people we meet are either walking their dogs or harvesting seaweed in wetsuits and goggles. They look at Dean's camera in puzzlement.

Dean snaps a shot of the seaweed gatherers and remarks, "This tsunami wall is only half the height of the waves that washed over those towns up north. With their history of tsunami, it's no wonder the Japanese don't face their windows toward the sea." We both look inland toward Ellen's apartment building, clearly visible from where we are standing, and catch each other's pensive expressions.

Without comment, we head back toward the school for the opening ceremony.

The Tohaku Junior High students, in naval-like uniforms, are kneeling on the wooden floor in severely straight rows in the unheated gymnasium. On stage at the microphone, the school principal reads a letter from the prime minister. Ellen is translating for us where we are standing on the overhead balcony.

The prime minister's message is sobering. He reminds the children that many young people their age have died, and that it is now up to them to step up and assist the country in the recovery effort. It is vitally important that they each study hard and do their best in all their work. This letter takes fifteen minutes to read; afterward the principal reiterates all the points. By the end, we are all feeling pale.

The students stand and sing the school song, which Ellen roughly translates as "rising high above Mount Daisen, where the Tohaku school shines with power and might, . . . etc." Their young voices are disciplined and clear, in a performance with no audience except their teachers and us two Americans.

When they finish, there is no applause. The principal returns to the microphone and indicates our presence above them. He informs them that Ellen Sensei's parents have brought a gift from American children, and the entire student body turns their faces curiously in our direction. With Ellen's prompting, Dean and I stoop and pick up the long strings of folded cranes and hold them above our heads, the ends dangling to the floor.

In unison, in silence, every one of the Tohaku Junior High students bows to us.

28

The Inside of the Pot

Jane

We are back in the United States though not yet home, waiting for our delayed connecting flight to arrive. All the signs are in English, the toilets need no instructions, and I have gobbled down a tasty sandwich with cheese. The baggage carousels stopped revolving more than twenty minutes ago, and the only other people in the area are slumped in their plastic chairs without anticipation.

The seats across from me back up to a stainless steel wall, so I shift over there. Now I have a place to lean my head. Reaching into my pocket, I draw out a ruby-red string of rosary beads and cradle them between my fingers. I have heard it said, "As long as one person in a family prays, that will be enough." I'm not sure exactly what this means, but it seems like a good general philosophy of parenting that isn't a whole lot of trouble, so why not?

Especially why not if one has just left a daughter in a country devastated by an earthquake, a tsunami, and a nuclear crisis? The morning we left Japan, the news reported that the Tokyo Electric Power Company was pumping nitrogen gas into the reactors at the Daiichi plant to prevent another hydrogen explosion like those that happened after the tsunami.

I am praying for Ellen, of course, but not just for her. In the last ten days, I have met and learned to care about many people who live on that troubled island on the other side of the world. Junko and her beautiful family are forever in my heart and my prayers. The Miyamoto family graced us with an invitation to their home and gave us fine hand-thrown pottery, explaining to us that in Japanese pottery, it is the inside of the dish that matters, not the outside. The Ellen-kai children climbed into Dean's lap and pulled at his mustache without fear, and the Manabi Eikaiwa ladies, who learned the Ten Commandments, treated us to a traditional Japanese meal.

They are all in my prayers, but the person I am most grateful for is Ellen's supervising teacher, Ito Sensei. He welcomed us with his British-accented English, Japanese bow, and delighted smile. He spoke with respect for us and praised our daughter as if she were his own. "I want you to know that Ellen Sensei has been a pleasure to work with at Tohaku Junior High. She has probably not told you, but the volunteer work she does has earned her much respect among the entire faculty."

Dean and I smiled at this with more pride than we could disguise. "You could not have told us anything that would make us happier," we assured him.

These lovely Japanese people have shown me that it was wrong of me to think that I had failed at passing on my faith tradition. For if our daughter knows that it is important to give of herself, her time, her friendship, and her love, what else could we have taught her? If she knows and lives these things, and she prays over all of it, how could she not know God?

In Japan I have listened much and learned more.

Now, in the airport praying over all this, I lean my head back against the wall, close my eyes, find my place on the beads, and begin murmuring the Apostles' Creed. From there I move on to the Our Father, the Glory Be, Oh, My Jesus, and eventually to the serenity of ten Hail

Marys. At each decade the sequence repeats, and soon I have lost track
of time, place, and modern travel inconveniences.

A man's voice begins humming on the periphery of my awareness.
I open my eyes to see a slightly built janitor poking his broom under
the chairs next to mine. I lift my feet for him and ask, "Would you like
me to move?"

"No, Ma'am, not necessary."

After he sweeps around me, he glances at the glittery string in my
hands and says helpfully, "There's an outlet 'round the end of that post
if you need to recharge that thing."

29

Lessons Learned

Ellen

The underside of the picnic table in the school's middle courtyard has a lot of black fungus growing on it. This is my first realization as I crouch underneath it, ducking my head to keep the black ick from getting in my hair. My second realization is that I am not crouching correctly. The three JHS girls under the table with me demonstrate the appropriate "take cover" posture, and I correct myself.

"Oops, thanks."

All around the courtyard I can see students and faculty huddled in doorways and under sturdy structures. The school principal and head teachers are scurrying about with clipboards and bullhorns, making sure we are all taking this seriously. Today's earthquake drill has been on the schedule for weeks, with all points thoroughly reviewed and re-reviewed. Everyone knows where we should go and what we should do.

What was not broadcast was the time of the drill. Even I was caught off guard when the alarm sounded during recess. By having it during the thirty-minute break, the administrators have assured that there will be plenty of time for the procedure without having to sacrifice any class time. The teachers think this is a masterstroke of genius.

The students think this is cruel and unusual.

Vice Principal Okamoto's voice comes over the PA system, "The 'earthquake' has finished. Please, proceed with evacuation to the school grounds."

There are sighs of relief as we stand from our cramped positions, but otherwise it is silent as 400 students and staff stream out from the building and onto the sports practice ground. With an ease born from hundreds of similar assemblies, the students split themselves into grade, class, gender, and height, sitting down on the ground only when everyone is present. Line leaders run forward to their homeroom teachers and report in, and the teachers inform the head teacher of the year. Head teachers wait until everyone in the grade is accounted for and then report to Mr. Okamoto.

My job is to take pictures for the faculty to review later. I dutifully snap multiple shots of the orderly lines, making sure to get the school in the background to add a little artistry. A few of the students grimace at me, obviously not pleased to be sitting on the hard, dusty ground. I can do no more than shrug and smile. We have to maintain silence, as if this was a real emergency evacuation.

Practice makes perfect.

Pleased with the speed and orderliness of the building evacuation, one of the teachers steps forward. "Right. That concludes the earthquake portion of the drill. Next we'll begin the tsunami drill. As you know this is new, so pay attention."

The students perk up, a few lean forward slightly to mumble to their neighbors. "Quiet!" three teachers bark in unison. "You have to listen!" A head teacher rolls her eyes at me. "They're such children," she mutters. "When will they ever grow up?"

I decide this isn't a good time to mention that student behavior on par with this would be unimaginable during an American tornado drill. As I recall, we spent a lot of time throwing gravel at one another.

Now that the riotous mumbling has been squelched, the teacher continues with his instructions. "We will proceed. Third-year boys; you know what to do?" The four long lines of fifteen-year-olds nod. "Good, everyone else will stay seated. Third years, you may go."

As one, fifty-plus teenage boys stand up, and in their lines, jog off the school grounds. Curious, I follow behind, camera at the ready. Principal Ishiga is running beside me, his camera also out to document the event.

"Where are we going exactly?" I ask, watching as the boys run down a slight incline and head north toward the ocean.

"To Midori preschool," Mr. Ishiga informs me. Sure enough, the first of the boys turn at the gate of the small private preschool two blocks down the street. The teachers there have obviously been expecting them as they hold the gate open to allow easier entry.

"Oh?" I teach at both schools and know that occasionally the older students will volunteer with the little ones as part of their community outreach requirement. Why they would be going there today though . . .?

"In the recent Tohoku disaster, one preschool was saved only because the junior high school students took it upon themselves to help bring the children to higher ground," Mr. Ishiga reminds me. "We've decided to create a plan to do the same, should such an occurrence happen here."

"And the boys are the fastest and strongest," I finish for him. Down the street, the boys have started to exit the preschool. Each is leading a tiny toddler by the hand.

The preschoolers are all wearing quilted hoods to protect them from falling debris. They toddle along, clutching the hands of their "big brothers." Some of them are wildly excited, skipping along and chattering to their rescuers. Others are shy, hesitant to go along with this strange game.

As the parade continues, two preschool teachers brush past me, carrying a hood that fell off one young tike. Distracted, it takes me a moment to focus again when a group of four comes into view. The boy on the left is doing fine, walking in a half crouch, encouraging the little girl to follow. The boy at the right is struggling. I know the girl he's walking with, and I can see she's totally distracted by her hood and perhaps overwhelmed by the whole experience. As I step forward to help, the boy on the left turns, and I realize it's Akira.

Akira—smart, angry, mercurial, and suddenly, gentle. Extending his free hand, he offers it to the child, speaking softly. She stares a moment, then grasps it. Now, safe between two big brothers, she walks forward more confidently, and Akira faces forward, a smile on his face I've never seen before. Both boys nod at me as they pass.

More students return, some of them now carrying babies. It's easy to see which ones have younger siblings at home as they bounce the infants in their arms with an easy familiarity. Even the only children are rising to the occasion, forgoing their usual rough chaos for soft voices and reassuring smiles.

I find myself next to their head teacher again and notice she's as dumbstruck as I am. The sight before us is so utterly at odds with what we've come to expect from this group of kids. Where is the complaining? The threats? The disobedience?

She shakes her head, as if to clear it. "Unbelievable. We should ask the preschool if we can borrow the babies every day."

I nod silently. There is an undeniable magic here, but I find myself wondering if it's coming from the toddlers or the teens. It may be, I think, that the lamb was not the gentler of the two animals. Perhaps it was the lion all along.

30

The Virgin Mary in My Zen Garden

Jane

The real sin against life is to abuse and destroy beauty, even one's own—even more one's own, for that has been put in our care and we are responsible for its well-being.
—Katherine Anne Porter

The spruce tree in front of our house had to come down. Its fifty-foot height rubbed the shingles on the roof, and its roots were growing under the slab foundation, which meant there were issues from the tips of its needles to far beneath the earth. But it was a magnificent tree, and it's troubling to be the destroyer of beauty. Dean reluctantly hired a company to chop down the tree, but in a fit of unfocused remorse, he wouldn't let them grind out the stump. So, ten feet in front of our brick ranch, we have an uneven mass of stump, roots, and prickly pine needles stretching twenty feet in either direction.

This pretty much describes Dean's position, too, at this stage of his career. The same economic slump that sent our daughter searching for work in the Far East has bitten into Dean's company, a contract research organization in the pharmaceutical industry. Business is uncertain, workers are nervous, and though it's hardly a tsunami, it is discouraging. He comes home from work worried, frustrated, and frayed. He doesn't complain because he still has a job, and many of our

friends do not. There is no space to complain when so many are hurt-
ing. We don't live all that far from Detroit.

After our return from Japan, a simmering idea emerges in my
mind that involves both our tree stump and the economic slump. The
landscape in Tottori Prefecture is a challenging one, with mountains,
oceans, waterfalls, and endless rocks. The scenery has left me smit-
ten with the Zen-garden concept of asymmetrical shrubs surrounded
by concentric circles of combed pebbles. One afternoon in early summer, I show Dean some photos of Japanese Zen gardens and sketch
out a simple plan to cover our stump with a soothing, Mount Fuji-
like cone of pebbles surrounded by miniature junipers and creeping
thyme. Dean is a chemist not a landscaper, but out of affection for me,
he takes my sketch and drives to the local garden shop.

All summer, while Ellen protects us with optimistic reports of the
Japanese government's plan to dissipate environmental radiation by
planting acres of sunflowers, Dean is planting shrubbery and raking
little pebbles. He places stepping stones over the spruce roots and
transplants Japanese iris and American wintergreen.

When it is complete, after weeks of digging and weeding, we sit
side by side in a modified lotus position and contemplate the patterns
of the stones. It is nice, but something is missing. "We need a Virgin
Mary statue," I say.

He glances at me. "We do? How big? Not like the one on I-94,
I hope?"

"No, no. Like so—." I measure about twelve inches with my hands.

Dean is silent for a minute or two. "I've always wanted you to be
the best Catholic you can be. If you want a Mary statue, go ahead."

I hug his arm. It's true what he says. My good Lutheran husband has
always supported my chosen spiritual path, as I have supported his. He
is a committed Lutheran who has been faithful to what his ancestors
passed on to him. I would not change that part of him because of the

great value I put on my own struggle to remain faithful to what I've been taught. We belong to both congregations and occasionally attend together. When we go to our separate churches, we always share the different takes on the sermons of the day. There are crucifixes throughout our home, and our daughters sing hymns in four-part harmony. Dean is an associate member of the St. Vincent de Paul Society, and for many years I was a member of the library committee at the Lutheran church.

If Christian unity has a chance of becoming reality, it might start with families like ours. It is this complex kind of unity that has produced our complex daughters. And after this whole Japanese adventure, we are only beginning to find out what it will be like to support them in their spiritual paths.

After a few moments, Dean says, "What we need is fifteen rocks."

"Hmm?"

"Those Zen gardens all had fifteen large rocks, spaced carefully so that the person meditating would not be able to see all of them at once."

"Why is that?" I ask.

He shrugs. "You're the Catholic; meditation is your specialty, not mine."

"Stones," I correct him. "Not rocks, stones."

He has a puzzled look. "What's the difference?"

"A rock is what you find in the wild. Once you pick it up and use it for something, it becomes a stone. For instance: We would say that we follow a rocky path, but we say we build a stone church. You throw a stone, but you trip over a rock."

He gives me a sideways grin. "I thought of a name for your garden."

"*Your* garden, too—you built it."

"What do you think about calling it Henri?"

I squint at him, confused. "Henri, the garden?"

"Yeah, after one of your favorite authors, Henri Nouwen."

I wait for it.

He nods, pleased with himself. "It will be your Nouwen Zen Garden."

31

Almost Ready to Go

Ellen

"I bought extra water and granola bars, and Tamiko says we can take her car. It'll get better mileage than any of ours." Will's voice comes through my cell phone. "You can leave yours parked in our driveway while we're gone."

"Great, thanks." I'm scrolling through my e-mail searching for the correspondence I need. "Oh, here it is! Angela, the main contact from **O.G.A.**, the aid agency we will be working for, says they should have a room we can use, but we'll all have to bunk together. Is that okay with you and Matt?"

"You know we'd never turn down a chance like that!" Will jokes, laughing at my grumbled response. "C'mon El, I'm teasing you. We're eager to get up there. We'd sleep in the car if we had to."

"Yeah, I know," I assure him. "Angela also says we need to arrange for our own volunteer insurance. Do you think we can do that at the town hall?"

"Already got it," Will confirms. "Matt signed up for his when he applied for the official volunteer leave from his town. It's inexpensive and shouldn't take more than twenty minutes."

A mere twenty minutes for an application process is almost unheard of in Japan. I'm relieved. "Great. I'll go tomorrow. My supervisor has already been up north twice to volunteer, so he said he'd go with me to file the paperwork."

"You know," Will says, "the fact that this group needs us to set up our own insurance is a good sign they'll have us doing actual work. Not just this drive-around-and-sort-stuff some of the full-package volunteer agencies are offering. It's a good sign."

"Yeah . . ." This is what I want to do, I remind myself. I want to actually volunteer. Whatever that means.

Ever since the earthquake and tsunami destroyed the coast of Tohoku, I've been seized by a need to travel there to help. I'm not sure how much of this urge is a need to see it for myself, and how much of it is a pure volunteering spirit, but I'm giving my motives the benefit of the doubt.

My first chance came in May when a group of similarly minded English teachers from around Japan reached out to me through Facebook. I was a click away from joining the expedition when the news reported a new spike in radiation around the Fukushima Daiichi plant, and I pulled out. Wouldn't want to unnecessarily worry the parents, right? That'd be irresponsible.

And despite being an invincible twenty-five-year-old, I'm not so sure nuclear radiation falls under the list of things that couldn't possibly happen to me.

Now it's August and I'm going. No, seriously, I'm totally going this time. I have to. I already asked for the time off school and told them I was going. Now that other people have praised my bravery I can't back out. I may have left it till too late as it is. Five months is a long time—what if they've already cleared up all the rubble? Gotten all the boats back in the water where they belong? I know these thoughts are horribly misguided, but still . . .

I won't be going alone, which is a huge relief. I've joined forces with two JET colleagues. Will is a teacher in Hojo Town, and Matt is the coordinator of international relations in nearby Yurihama.

Will is a tall, slim, red-haired Australian, who married his lovely wife, Tamiko, a few weeks after the disaster in March. He's quiet, with a self-deprecating sense of humor and an impressive knowledge of obscure trivia and '80s music. With his recent marriage, he's become happy, no longer focused solely on his job teaching at a local high school, having finally found a girl who loves him for his quirky sense of humor and gentle ways.

Matt is dark-haired, sardonic, pale-skinned—and no stranger to Pacific Island living, having lived many years in Hawaii. He's studied Japanese his whole life and moves through his office with a natural ease and suaveness that I can't even begin to muster. Highly intelligent and often critical, he and Will love to delve into philosophical and political discussions.

And then there's me: a talkative, determinedly happy, accidental English teacher. I like meeting people, exclaiming about things, and listening to light-hearted pop music. Driving the length of Japan's main island together should be tons of fun.

Actually, now that a volunteer organization has agreed to take us on, the work boots have been purchased, and the departure date has been set, I'm pretty nervous. It has only now occurred to me that I have no experience, and by extension, no useful skills that can be applied in a disaster zone. What am I going to do? Emote over the rubble?

Matt and Will have never done anything like this either, but out of the three, I'm definitely the weak link. Both of them are a few years older, better at Japanese, and physically stronger than I am. I won't be able to best them at anything, which bothers me. Maybe if we're required to sing? Nah, that's never gonna happen . . .

For the first time ever, I regret not taking a single welding class.

I'm also worried I won't be able to handle being in an area of devastation. I've never had to face such a situation before. For all I know, I'll be emotionally hamstrung the moment I get there. I worry that I'll be so useless that I'll become part of the problem. That would be the ultimate failure.

Now, as I pack my duffel bag with ratty T-shirts and cargo pants, I wish someone had written a how-to book for volunteering. Something that would give me a clue as to how to survive this self-imposed challenge and maintain composure in a situation I'm underqualified for. Maybe there's something on the Internet? Oh, wait . . .

My mom already wrote that book.

Since I left America for Asia, my mother has become an author. I've been removed from the transformation, having only seen the pieces of it that make their way onto the Internet and into our Skype sessions. I'm proud of her, and I read the book, but because I grew up hearing those stories around the dinner table, it wasn't exactly a revelation seeing them written down. Now that I think about it though, that whole book is about volunteering.

I leave my packing unfinished on the floor and go to find my signed copy. Guess it's time to start listening to my mom . . .

32

"I Read Your Book Again"

Jane

It is a chicken salad lunch again, but today I'm not the speaker. There is one talk scheduled for tonight, another in the morning, and the third speech tomorrow afternoon. This is the meal when I can eat all the food I want without worrying about burping into the microphone, so I am enjoying it. The location is a Jesuit college, and I am staying in the priests' residence on campus, a dorm-like two-story building with an open kitchen and a chapel nearby. Perfect.

My lunch companions are mostly retired Jesuit priests because the younger ones have gone off to work. These men keep the world in balance with their conversation alone. For instance, television never comes up, but they know exactly what is happening on the ground in Egypt, Sudan, and West Virginia. They discuss the Notre Dame football team and local food pantry shortages. Last week, Karl Rove was the scheduled speaker on campus, and this week, it's me, a volunteer at a thrift store.

Fr. Tom is the least talkative of the lot, but he has a life story that intrigues me. When the others have finished and left the table, I ask him what it was like to live out west for twenty years on a Native American reservation.

He smiles gently. "Mostly, I just followed the tribal elder around."

"Where did he go?"

"The people were generally Catholics, but they were spread out all over the place in small communities. This elder—he was Catholic, too—travelled to their villages, and I would go along and celebrate Mass, and then they would all line up to talk to him. After we listened to their troubles, we would pray over them for whatever needed healing."

"Healing?"

"You see, Jane, for them, religion and healing are the same thing: spiritual healing, emotional healing, relationship healing, and physical healing—they are all based in God. That's why their religious leaders are also their healers."

I am fascinated. "Did you see any healings while you were there?"

"All the time."

"What kind?"

"'The lame will walk and the deaf will hear' kind of healings. It was the real thing. The first time, when we laid our hands on a person, and they were cured, I was like, Whoa there—did that just happen? My friend shook his head at me and said, 'Father, you got to have faith.'"

I ponder anew this small priest and then ask him, "So, back up a minute. How does healing work?"

"Well, it's God who heals them—their *faith* in God is what heals them. Our part is mostly listening, Jane. It always starts with listening. My friend and I would listen to their stories, let them tell us about the pain in their lives, and then we would pray over them. We could lay on hands or sprinkle holy water or burn sage and incense, but that was after the listening, after allowing them to tell their stories and name the problem. Then, if they believed that God could heal them, and that he wanted to heal them, that's how it could happen."

After this awakening conversation with Fr. Tom, I begin to ponder how desperately the nation of Japan needs healing, all kinds of healing. And anyone, like my daughter, who is living through the recovery period, must necessarily require healing too. But how do I listen to her? She is so far away . . .

On our next Skype date, she mentions that she has signed up to volunteer in the disaster zone. The Fukushima plant is still steaming away, but I push back those worries. Instead, I work on controlling my facial expression and try to listen.

"I read your book again," she says. "It was better the second time."

She cannot know how startling this statement is to me. "It was? Why?"

"Well, I'm going up north to volunteer and help these people who have lost everything: their homes, their jobs, their possessions, their loved ones. Some of them have lost their whole world. And this makes me nervous because I don't have any idea what they're going through or what I can possibly do to help them."

"I see what you mean. When all the news is bad, where do you begin?"

"Exactly. So I read your book again because I realized that you didn't know what you were doing either. When you started volunteering at the thrift store, you were clueless about how to help those people."

I can't help but laugh. "That was pretty much the case."

"So when I read the book the second time, I wasn't looking at the stories, I was hoping for a help-line." She pauses. "Tell me if I have this right: at the thrift store you spend a lot of time, maybe most of the time, just listening to their stories. You don't know what to tell them, but they end up giving you some amazing wisdom. And then they can start to turn things around. Is that how it works?"

I am nodding, holding back my emotions by holding back the words.

"What else do I need to know?"

"Pray," I answer. "I know you pray already, but you're going to need a lot of prayer."

"When I get a chance . . ."

"Pa and I will be praying too. Remember that you can't save anybody. God saves people—you don't. The help you give involves just going to them, doing what you can, and listening. You're exactly the right person for this. I'm so proud of you."

33

Water Ranger

Ellen

"Angela says it's fine if we're late," I inform Will and Matt, slipping my phone into one of the pockets of my cargo pants. "She says the traffic usually backs up at this exit because residents need to get their IDs validated to avoid the toll road fees."

"Good of the government to exempt them," Will says as Matt manages to steer us through the auto-pay lane. "GPS says to turn right once you get down this ramp, Matt."

Matt shrugs. "Traffic is moving slow, not as bad as the Osaka backup though." Since he's the driver for this leg of the trip, he plugs in his iPod and puts on an NPR broadcast.

I sigh and slouch in the backseat, ready to be out of this car and doing something. After fourteen hours, one business hotel, and countless gas-station stops, I'm willing to admit that Japan, though not any bigger than California, is still a really long country. A blue traffic sign comes into view as we inch forward, and I sit up and say, "Guys, look at the sign."

It's a standard highway sign, blue where its American counterpart would be green, arrows pointing out which way to turn for which city. But the place names on this particular sign have captured my attention. Should we turn left, we will reach Kesennuma and Motoyoshi. Kesennuma has been all over the news for months, the name now synonymous with "tsunami." Motoyoshi doesn't even exist anymore, as it was the town closest to sea level. But the GPS told us to turn right, and going right will lead us to Minamisanriku.

Minamisanriku was a fishing and resort town, with most buildings and businesses located close to the waterfront. The town was prepared for a tsunami with eighty predetermined evacuation sites. But not even the imaginations of the most sea-weathered fishermen could have anticipated the fifty-two-foot wave that destroyed 95 percent of the town, submerging thirty-one of the evacuation spots in seconds.

In the days following the disaster, half the 19,000 residents of Minamisanriku were reported missing. Though the number has fluctuated in the following months, thousands remain unaccounted for. The Japanese government hasn't released revised figures yet. The reality is, these numbers account for just one town, and the Japanese government is struggling to cope with the same situation in every city up and down the coast for hundreds of miles.

We've cleared the traffic jam and are rolling past rice fields when Will points. "Look. The pavement is cracked." We all crane forward to see our first evidence of earthquake damage. It soon becomes not one crack but many, and the ride becomes rougher. Matt starts to steer more carefully.

"It shouldn't be too much longer now, the sign back there said, oh . . ." He trails off, and all we can do is gape as the view before us becomes a wholly different world.

The cracks in the road aren't even a talking point anymore. *Everything* around us is cracked. We can see exactly how far the wave came inland because the first fifty feet of trees on the sides of the mountains are dead and brown. The salt water must have killed their root systems. Piles of mangled cars are stacked on top of each other in the middle of fields. Fields with no buildings in them, only foundations. The buildings that are still standing look like the bombed-out photos of post-war Europe. I gasp as we drive past a gutted apartment building. A car balances neatly on the roof, a torn cloth trailing down from beneath one of its tires.

Matt has to slow his speed to a crawl since it's impossible to avoid potholes. Will starts to snap a few pictures before motioning to the left and saying in a hushed voice, "There's the government building, the one in all the broadcasts. See it?"

It's hard to miss the forlorn red iron scaffolding, all that remains of the city's Disaster Management Center. The Japanese press widely reported how the only survivor, the town's mayor, climbed the radio antenna at the top of the building to survive, barely maintaining his grasp as the wave submerged him for almost three minutes. It has become a pilgrimage site of sorts, with both residents and tourists leaving flowers at its base.

It's not all death. The cell phone provider Softbank has managed to set up an emergency store and tower in the midst of all this mess. And to the left is a hastily constructed convenience store, advertising ice and vegetables. There is no lack of cars on the road, though everyone drives in the same erratic way, avoiding standing pools of water and boats.

Huge seagoing ships are sitting in the middle of the road, with no one paying them much attention. Maybe that's why I can't stop staring. How does one go about removing them? Whose boats are they? Are the owners even alive to claim them?

Aside from being unsure about whether it's okay to take pictures, I'm surprised at my own lack of reaction. Apparently, my brain has slipped into accepting this as my current reality. I'm not flipping out or crying—I'm just ready to get out of this car. My wishes are answered as we finally reach the small mountainside preschool where we'll be staying. As we pull into the parking lot, four people lounging on the back of a moving truck wave us over. Everyone meets in the middle, shaking hands and exchanging what pleasantries we can manage while sizing each other up.

Angela is everything I imagine Lara Croft Tomb Raider would be in real life. She's fiercely beautiful, with a no-nonsense ponytail and steel-toed boots that are worn because of use, not design. The straps and buckles on her clothing are being used for tools and radios. I've never seen a more competent-looking person in my life.

Peter, her second-in-command, is muscled, with an eyebrow piercing and an impatient energy. We find out later he was on the cusp of starting his career as a mixed martial arts fighter in Tokyo before the disaster. Now he tills fields and uses his enormous strength to carry water pallets.

Choki is a local fisherman, with skin like leather and a smile like the sun. With no boat, decimated seabeds, and lack of a job, he now devotes all his hours to restoring his community. He will be our local guide and translator. I'm quickly realizing that the northern dialect sounds like an entirely different language.

Stephen is the friendliest, and the happiest to see us. He's a fellow volunteer up from Tokyo, and has spent the last week with these three. He seems pleased not to be the newest member of the group anymore.

"We already lost an hour waiting for you guys, so we won't go to the fields today," Peter informs us. "We'll deliver water to the temporary housing developments instead."

Angela eyes us. "You said you all have driver's licenses, right? *Japanese* driver's licenses?" We all nod. "Awesome. Peter and I are from Tokyo, so we can't drive. We really need you to drive our trucks so Choki can have a break. Can anyone drive a stick?" We quickly determine that Will can drive the manual truck, and the rest of us split up between vehicles.

The morning passes in a blur of work. As we visit each cramped hilltop encampment, we park the truck in a central "street" and work our way up and down the rows of identical, prefabricated aluminum-sided shelters. The shelters are clean, orderly, and heart-achingly lived in. Small dogs bark at us from some, beautiful flower pots decorate the steps of others. We visit each briefly, knocking on the door to inform them that we've left bottled water on their doorstep, and then move on to the next one. The pallets are heavy. I can't handle more than two at a time, but I watch in amazement as Peter takes two on each arm.

"Do the temporary apartments not have running water?" I ask Angela, as I wait at the truck for Matt to hand down my next load.

"No, they do. But the emergency pipelines that run along the coast are just propped up on sandbags," she tells me, checking her watch. "So small rocks and dirt still come through the water supply all the time. It's no good for the kids."

Oh. I lean back to balance the weight of my water bottles and trudge down another row. As I drop off the second one with a cheerful greeting, a small boy pokes his head out the sliding door leading into his family's main room. "Oh, Mommy, there's a foreigner out here!" He calls back into the house.

"Well, say, 'hello'," she instructs him. "You know how."

He jumps down onto the gravel in front of me, slipping into a pair of red sneakers. "Bonjour!" he offers.

I stare at him in astonishment. He can't be more than four years old. "No, not 'bonjour,'" I tell him in Japanese.

He thinks for a moment. "Hola?"

I shake my head, grinning. "Nope . . ."

His face brightens. "Hello!" he cries triumphantly, rewarded by my laugh. "Mommy, she speaks English!" he calls into the house.

An apologetic face appears around a corner. "I'm so sorry. He's been learning from so many aid workers."

"No, not at all," I reassure her. "He's so smart." I admire his T-shirt. "Wow, what a cool shirt—is that a Power Ranger?"

"No way. This is Kamen Rider!" he informs me indignantly. "I can do his moves—watch!" Suddenly I'm sucked into his game in which he is clearly the hero and I am some sort of monster.

We battle our way back down the row, stopping only when I break some unstated game rule. "Monsters can't transform," he tells me. "Only I can transform! I'm Kamen Rider, remember?"

I apologize for stepping outside of my scaly monster boundaries. When his mother comes over to join us, she admonishes him, "Now, now, you have to leave the nice girl alone. She needs to work."

"Oh, it wasn't a problem." I assure her that my aching arms have thoroughly enjoyed the break. "It was lots of fun playing with you," I tell him.

"Are you gonna come back and play with me again?" he asks.

"I . . . well, if I can," I say, not sure if I'll ever have the chance to. "Here, give me a high five." He does so, and his mother scoops him up to carry him back home. I wave until he disappears inside.

Angela appears out of nowhere. "Good work," she observes.

"What? Oh, sorry. I was a monster, and we were playing," I rush to explain, knowing I've slacked off on an entire row of apartments. "I teach at a preschool in Kotoura, and he's Kamen Rider, you see . . ."

"No, it's good," she tells me, swinging up into the open back of the truck as Choki starts the engine. "The kids need someone to play with. That's important too. If you want to take pictures with the kids, that's fine. We never have enough for the website."

I jog behind the truck as it heads to the next grouping of buildings. Apparently, being a monster has fulfilled my brief for the day.

Is this really volunteering?

34

Ready to Listen

Jane

Do we teach our children about God so that they will stay close to him?

Even if he is in the middle of a disaster zone?

I am lighting a ton of candles this week, which is made easier because I'm in church more than usual because of the Feast of the Assumption. Ellen called us once after she arrived in the tsunami zone, but we haven't heard from her since.

The first-aid organization that she contacted asked if she would volunteer to chauffeur scientists into the crippled nuclear plant each day. She refused and told them to find someone who was past her child-bearing years. We haven't heard what her new assignment will be.

Her birthday is this week, and I sent her a package, but it is probably sitting in her apartment until she returns. We can't Skype because she doesn't have access to the Internet. There doesn't seem to be any way for me to help her, except to pray.

One consolation is that she is not alone. She travelled to the tsunami zone with like-minded friends, and they are working for an established organization. Something I have learned from years of volunteering is that working in a group is both humbling and dynamic. With many people involved, there is little need for heroics and along with that, many possibilities for unexpected success. A community can achieve heights that no individual could ever reach. The mechanics of social interactions are no different for faith-based groups than for secular groups. Just like junior high, there are bullies, broken hearts, rivalries, shame, and love.

Ellen knows all this because Dean and I have modeled volunteering her entire life. We've also told her all the grace stories and pointed her to the source of our inspiration and strength. Apparently, she was listening.

Now, Ellen is volunteering as part of a community. And God is certainly with her and with them. He is always in the disaster zones of this world.

I can't wait to hear her stories.

35

Feast of the
Assumption Birthday

Ellen

We pile into the front of the truck with Peter. "Today's going to be hot," he tells us, as we fill up on gasoline at the gas station across from the destroyed hospital. "We'll have to buy some frozen water bottles at the 7-Eleven." He follows my gaze to the gaping holes in the side of the building. "The wave carried the patients right out of the building on their beds," he says. "There wasn't anything anyone could do."

As Matt guides our truck down what has become the main route through the debris field, we pass a group of volunteers sorting through rubble next to where their tour bus is parked. It's simply by chance that we've joined up with O.G.A. and have been given the opportunity to stay in the town and help with this mission. By "stay" I mean share a room built for two with four people, ignore the sewage in the bathroom, and hang our bucket-washed clothes on the fence outside. But hey, at least it has air conditioning when the power is on.

Our mission is farming. That's right, we're not knocking down houses or clearing roads—it's good old-fashioned agriculture. Miyagi Prefecture, where Minamisanriku is located, has the most unused farmland in the entire country. A hundred years ago, this area had been an agricultural economy. But as the locals discovered they could make more money faster through fishing, thousands of acres fell into disuse, abandoned for the wealth of fish beneath the ocean waves.

The tsunami has forced people to rethink. Not only did the wave wipe out the towns, but the shifting earth plates dropped the level of the coast by up to five feet in places. This has destroyed the fishing beds, driven the fish away, and ended the livelihood of many.

We're given chainsaws, weed whackers, and a tractor, and pointed toward the area that needs to be cleared. It's backbreaking, eye-irritating, occasionally perilous work. An hour in, we discover a forgotten well—if nearly losing the tractor down an uncovered well shaft can be counted as discovery. With some inventive use of our newly chopped lumber and strategically placed man power, we manage to save the tractor.

Out in the reclaimed fields, for the umpteenth time I yank the dust mask away from my nose and mouth, trying to get a breath of air that doesn't smell like sour felt. It's a bad idea since I haven't waited for the latest cloud of quick lime to settle and I succumb to a coughing fit. Sighing in frustration, I glance down at my clothes, covered in the gritty white muck. This will have to be the fashion statement I'm making today.

Between the large protective goggles, the dust mask, the gloves, and the work boots, I'm sure I'm quite a sight. But everyone else looks exactly the same. Matt raises an eyebrow at me as he passes with the push mower. "That's a good look, Knuth. Don't know why you didn't try it sooner."

"Oh, you know," I joke, brushing myself off, "I thought I'd try out something new, since it's my birthday."

Stephen opens his eyes in surprise. "It's your birthday? Happy Birthday!"

"Thanks! I'm twenty-six years old," I say happily. "We're going to the restaurant in the hotel to celebrate. Want to join?"

"Yes, of course," Stephen says, calling across to Peter, "You in, Peter? It's Ellen's birthday!" Peter nods, and we all go back to our work, the image of refrigerated beer dancing on the edge of our thoughts.

Before the tsunami, Hotel Kanyo, located on the bay in Minamisanriku, was a five-star resort hotel, famous for its gorgeous view of the Pacific Ocean, the luxurious outdoor baths, and a delicious selection of local seafood. Though the building survived the earthquake without structural problems, the tsunami eviscerated the bottom five floors, including the outdoor baths. Equipped with backup generators, it was the only building in town with electricity and water. When the hotel manager realized this, he offered food and water until supplies started to run out. That's when O.G.A., originally formed as a one-off supply run, stepped in to bring food and water from Tokyo, which they have continued to do for the last five months.

At this point, the hotel has been completely restored, but the only paying guests are the ever-present media crews. The main money comes from the government, which pays the hotel to house more than eight hundred families not yet relocated to temporary housing. The hotel is like a small village, run by the same people who are now living in it. As volunteers, we have been given the privilege of using the beautiful hot springs baths to clean up in, and the opportunity to eat in the employee kitchen, should we wish. We use the bathing facilities eagerly but choose to pay for everything else, patronizing the café, the gift shop, and tonight, the small seafood restaurant.

As our work ends and the sun sets, we arrive back at the preschool where we're staying and grab our soap and a change of clothes. "Let's all meet in the lobby in an hour," Will suggests, and we split up, ready to get clean. My clothes smell of sweat, dirt, and lyme. It's really a whole new level of stench.

In Japan, one showers first, getting thoroughly clean and rinsed before ever entering the bathtub. The showers and baths are in two entirely different areas, and to bring any kind of soap into the hot springs portion would be unthinkable. I lost my shyness of public baths and shared nudity years before, especially since the baths are usually separated by sexes. If anything, it has given me a healthier body image, and I hardly even notice when the little girl at the shower next to me stares. Half an hour, and three hair scrubbings later, I feel cleansed enough to venture over to the outside baths.

There's no one else in the steamy pools tonight, and I stand alone, facing the ocean, with only a cliff face between me and the bay below. The sun has completely set, and in the quiet August night, I'm struck by the scene before me.

The ocean stretches out black and calm, the moon reflected in a silvery trail that seems to reach for me. The only light comes from the building behind me and from the stars. The whole area is in complete darkness. Far away in the hills I can see the shine coming from the surviving parts of the town, the mountaintop housing areas, but the lowlands are blanketed in a blue/purple shadow. *It's beautiful*, I think, and then immediately feel horrible.

Here I am, admiring the same ocean that killed thousands of people less than half a year before.

I forgive myself for my thoughts, it's my birthday after all. My birthday, August 15, the Japanese day of the dead. When I planned the volunteer trip to encompass this personally important day, I justified my decision by reminding myself that there's not really anything else to do on this day. Japan shuts down. May as well put myself to good use.

The waves lap gently at the rocks far below me, and I lean over the side of the rock pool to see them. I'm surprised to find the water full of flowers. Not just wildflowers, but beautiful bouquets, dozens of them, advancing and retreating with the tidal waters. They're not only directly below me, but all along the shore, as far as I can see. *How odd*, I think, and then the meaning hits me.

Thousands are still missing from Minamisanriku, and since the bodies haven't been found, must be presumed dead. During the Bon Festival, in which surviving family members are duty-bound to honor the deceased, the usual gathering spot is the graveyard, but those are gone too, washed out to sea. So these survivors, these bereaved, have no choice but to throw their offerings, with their love, into the ocean, hoping they will reach the resting place of their loved ones.

It takes my breath away.

At the arranged time, I meet my friends in the lobby, and we go into the restaurant together. The sight of the flowers has swept the joy right out of me, but I don't want to talk about it, so I smile, order an extravagant seafood bowl to support the local economy, and raise my beer to acknowledge their toasts to my health and happiness.

Good food and conversation take the edge off, and I'm about to order another beer when one appears at my elbow, held perfectly balanced on the tray by a handsomely dressed waiter. "Oh, thank you! I was just going to order another."

"This is for you, compliments of the gentleman at the bar," he informs me with a smile. "He heard it was your birthday and is happy you are celebrating it here with us."

All of us turn to see the man in question, and he raises his own beverage, nodding at Peter. "I know him," Peter says, raising a hand. "Local businessman, lives here with his family."

"But I . . . but he . . ." I stare at Peter. "He doesn't know me, I should be getting *him* a beer, shouldn't I?"

"Let him treat you," Peter observes, and I take the beer from the waiter. "They need something to celebrate, and your birthday is a good enough reason." At his cue I raise the beer in thanks, and my benefactor breaks into a wide grin.

This unexpected gift has made me feel even worse. I'm supposed to be helping these people, but here they are spending their money on me! I don't know why things are working out this way and yet . . . I sit back and watch as the man at the bar smiles at me again before turning to talk to the bartender.

Maybe I don't need to understand.

Maybe I should just celebrate my birthday.

36

Weeds

Ellen

I'm a morning person, but this morning has come far too early and with too much dew. I groan as I sit up in my lower bunk. Every muscle in my body screams. Now I understand why Matt is sleeping on the floor instead of in the upper bunk. My arms cannot even lift myself over the low guardrail meant to keep toddlers from rolling out of bed.

All this manual labor is taking a toll. Born into a privileged lifestyle in an economically prosperous country, I've never had to do much hard work, something my overused body is reminding me. The men wake up, and we all shuffle around, not speaking, not making eye contact.

It's the only way we can keep from admitting how hard this is.

Peter greets us as we make our way down to the trucks, looking as rock-solid as ever. We gather around him, nodding to Choki-san, who looks equally fit and unbothered.

"We've got a few things we could do today," Peter announces. "Choki is taking Stephen to the nearest station to catch a train home. For the rest of you, there's another field that needs some clearing, but it should only take two people. For the other two we've got a planted tomato field to be weeded, I thought I'd leave it up to—."

167

"I'll weed," I say quickly.

"Me, too." Will jumps in. "Weeding sounds good." We both look at Matt, who is glowering at us.

Hey, you gotta be quick.

Peter looks at the three of us for a moment then reconsiders. "How about we all weed?" he suggests, and some of the tension dissipates. "It's a big field, and we need the path up to it mown as well." With that decided, we divvy up driving responsibilities—it's my day to drive the big truck—and set out.

Today's location is on a mountain with a view of a cove which, judging by the number of building foundations, used to be heavily populated. Now it's all collapsed klaxon towers, shattered roof tiles, and driveways leading to nothing. The only house remaining is a beautiful example of Japanese countryside architecture, now standing alone on its mountain. The owners come out briefly to greet us and show us where to park and then disappear back inside.

The tomatoes are growing in a plot uphill from the house in long, neat rows that need attention. We set to work right away, happy to be doing anything that doesn't involve machinery.

The dirt feels warm beneath my knees and hands, and I fall into a comfortable rhythm, making sure to extract each root system as well as the leaves. It's another scorcher, but we stow our rapidly melting water bottles under the trees in the hopes that the water will remain somewhat cold.

Several hours in, I am crawling on my hands and knees toward the next plant when the ground trembles beneath me. I feel the tremors coming up through what should be solid rock, and freeze. It's over quickly though, and Peter doesn't even pause. "Not a big aftershock at all," he says. "The military helicopters didn't even fly out to look for a wave." We all adopt a faux blasé attitude to match his and go back to work.

Another hour passes before I trudge over to ask Peter a question. "Is there an outhouse here?"

He looks at me out of the corner of his eye. "Not at this site, no. We just go in the woods. If you can't, you can ask down at the house if they'll let you use their bathroom." With that he goes back to weeding.

I shrug and wander off into the woods. I was raised in Michigan. I've been camping. This won't be the first time I've peed behind a tree. Making sure I'm completely shielded from view, I drop trou and do my business. Minutes later I'm back in the field, determined to finish another two rows before the sun starts setting.

By the end of the day we've successfully weeded all the tomatoes. It's a real accomplishment, and I feel like dancing. Obvious results! Hooray! We're trying to get the encrusted dirt off our knees when Peter approaches us. "Good news. The family who lives here is having a cookout tonight with their son and some friends. They've asked us to join."

"Really? That's awesome, but we didn't bring anything."

"It's okay, just chip in some money for beer if you plan on drinking," Peter advises. Because I'm the designated driver, I stick to water, but the boys get right to it, cracking open a beer with the men as they get the small grills set up.

It's a smorgasbord of food: crab, octopus, fish, vegetables, and beautifully steamed rice. We can hardly believe our luck. To be asked to join the party is amazing, considering we're the only foreigners who've been working in the back field all day. The invitation is a huge honor.

I'm tired, so I pick a chair and settle down to listen. The men, all former fishermen, are complaining about the food. "This octopus is no good," one grumbles, cracking open a crab with his knife. "Where was it imported from? Hokkaido? Not the same level of quality as the Miyagi kind."

I eat silently, deciding this isn't the right time to say this is the best octopus I've ever tasted. It must be the way they've prepared it. These guys know what they're doing.

"You know, I had a call from a friend down near Kobe," says another. "Turns out that's where our fish migrated, can you believe it? He's from around here, so he recognized the type. He says the fishermen will give us a cut of the profits since they're Miyagi fish."

I'm pondering this information when I realize the oldest fisherman has taken the seat next to me and is talking. "Sorry, what was that?"

"You ever been in a tsunami?" he asks me again, and I shake my head. "I've been in three. Been a fisherman all my life, knew what was happening before most did."

"Really?" I set my chopsticks aside. "So what did you do?"

"Only way to survive a tsunami is to ride it out on the open sea," he says matter-of-factly. "Can't stay close to the shore or your boat will get damaged. The instant that earthquake was over, I grabbed my son, and we left port as fast as we could go."

"What happened?"

"Well, we rode it out, didn't we? I'm still the only one with my boat intact around here. But this was a big one, never seen anything like it. When we turned back for land, there was nowhere to go. No place to tie up, just debris. Dangerous water."

"So what did you do?" His old face is glowing in the light from the barbecue coals; I feel like I'm in a movie.

"We stayed on our boat for three days. Only had some snacks and one beer, not even the brand I like," he says. "Weren't any fish left to catch. Just black, dirty water."

We lapse into silence. I'm not brave enough to ask more about those three days. To wonder if they worried about those on land, to ask what else they saw in that black water. Finally, I think of a question that seems safe to ask. "What will you do now?"

"Now?" He laughs. "I'm a fisherman, weren't you listening? The government, they say they won't let us rebuild here. Politicians worried it's too dangerous, that it could happen again, but we won't listen to them. This is where I was born, this is where I'll stay."

"Aren't you scared?" I ask. "I mean, your house, it only just escaped didn't it?"

"Water came right up to the doorstep and then backed on down the mountain," he confirms. "Here's the thing; the ocean gave me my life." He motions toward his family, the food, his house. "All this I have because of the ocean, and so, if the ocean takes it away, I have to accept that." He nods into his chest. "That's the balance."

The evening ends when the beer runs out. We all pile back into the trucks, wave good-bye, and begin the tricky drive back to our preschool base camp. Peter is in a good mood, smiling at me as I inch the truck along the dark roads. "You did great today. I was impressed."

"Wha-really?" A small flower of pride blooms in my chest. "Thank you! It was a lot of weeds."

"Well, yeah, but what I meant was, we've never had a female volunteer actually go pee in the woods. They usually make a fuss and ask at the house, which really bugs the family. Not you though, you just peed like the boys."

The small flower of pride shrivels up and dies. "Oh, well . . . my family went camping a lot, I guess."

"You know what else is great," Will chimes in from the passenger seat. "You haven't put on any makeup all week."

"It's not like there's a reason to," I grumble. "We don't even have a mirror."

"Yeah, but most girls wouldn't do that," Will says cheerfully. "I'm impressed."

I sigh and concentrate on getting us all home safely, despite wanting to strangle them both. I had been dying to earn their respect and seem to have done so but . . . peeing in the woods? Really?

Men . . .

37

Release

Ellen

We've done it. Our time volunteering in the north has finished, blurring into a jumble of images, sounds, and muscle aches. We've handled farming, landscaping, charitable giving, truck driving, rubble clearing, amateur counseling, and team building with varying success. We've lived with each other in close quarters, endured smelling like barnyard animals, and behaved civilly to each other considering our polar-opposite approaches to life. Now, as we exit the McDonald's and climb into the car for the last thirty minutes of our journey, the last shreds of our goodwill are running out.

I settle into the back seat. "Almost home! Ugh, I can't believe I have to go into work tomorrow . . ."

Matt's head thumps back against the passenger seat headrest. "I cannot believe you are still talking." Will smiles and shifts the car into drive.

Oh, hell no. These two have been on the same side of every argument for the past 200 miles. I seriously cannot take any more of this "bro code" or whatever they think binds them. "Seriously, Matt? Is this just 'pick on Ellen' day?"

Will tries to intervene. "He's not picking on you, Ellen . . ."

"You wouldn't think so—you're as bad as he is! What do you call not telling me about the Starbucks at the rest stop in Osaka? You KNEW I'd been looking for one the whole way back."

Matt snorts. "I didn't think you'd be oblivious enough to miss it. Or that you'd hold a grudge all the way home."

"As if you two haven't been mad at me for buying that gourmet burger in Aichi."

Will glares at me in the mirror. "We'd been waiting to try those for hours."

"It's not my fault there was only one left."

"You could have at least told us before—."

"Why would I tell you? You wouldn't even sit at the same table as me when we went out for dinner with that volunteer group in Sendai!" To my horror I feel tears prickle at the corner of my eyes. I still don't know why they did that, leaving me to make friends with a table of Japanese businessmen.

"Because you're always so damn *peppy* everywhere we go!" Matt snarls. "Always have to be the bubbly one at the center of the conversation, don't you? Can't you just . . . turn off?!"

His remark steals my breath away for a moment, especially because Will says nothing, implying tacit agreement. "Maybe if you guys didn't abandon me to go hang out with cooler people!"

"I think . . ." Will attempts to mediate the rising conflict. "That we've just been in close quarters for quite a long time and—."

"Do not even try to be some kind of . . . of . . . neutral 'Switzerland' in this," I sneer. "It's not fooling anyone; you side with Matt 90 percent of the time and just talk all nice and quiet to calm me down!" That upset him, I can tell.

"I'm trying to be a gentleman."

"Bullshit."

Matt is laughing at my rage, and I childishly kick the back of his seat. "Shut up! You're such a jerk!"

"You pushed me to it," he informs me mockingly. "Along with most other guys, I'm sure."

Will holds up a hand. "Wait a second, Matt—."

"I hate you!"

"Feeling's mutual." We've arrived at his apartment, and Matt exits the car. "Will, I'll call you later this week. Ellen." He slams the door shut and walks away, shoulders stiff.

Will shifts the car into gear and waits until we're back on the road before testing the waters. "I think maybe we're all releasing some of the stress—."

"I hate him!" I wail and burst into tears.

Will chews nervously on his lip, not attempting to reopen conversation until we're pulling into the driveway where my car is parked. "Neither of you hate each other, you know. We're all just tired and . . ." He runs a hand through his hair. "You were kinda baiting him just then. But, yeah, Matt and I may have been ganging up on you a bit these last few days."

"I . . . I shouldn't have bought the last gourmet burger without telling you guys," I sob. "But, but I'm just so tired of trying to keep up with you two and . . ." I back into the shadows toward my car as the lights come on in the entryway of his house. "I'm gonna go home."

He glances toward the house. "Tamiko was saying she wants to have everyone over for a 'job well done' dinner later this week."

"No, I don't think . . ." I really just want to get out of here. "Thank Tamiko for me, but . . ."

"We should all maybe take a break from each other," Will agrees. He comes around the car to give me a quick hug. "Drive home safe, okay? We'll talk later."

I nod and hightail it back to Kotoura. Tears are rolling down my cheeks for half the drive, but I seem to have them under control as I arrive home at my apartment building. I can't even smell the normal stink of the green elevator carpet, possibly because the fumes rolling off my duffel bag are so noxious. I unlock the door of my apartment and collapse into the entryway.

Nothing has changed.

It's exactly how I left it: dirty dishes in the sink, scattered papers on the floor. I walk onto the balcony and look out on moonlit Kotoura. The first glance reminds me so much of Minamisanriku a shiver runs down my spine. There are the mountains, the ocean, the closely spaced houses. The only difference is that Kotoura is intact. Lights sparkle from every house; Tohaku Junior High school's grounds hold only neatly raked sand, not temporary housing structures.

I sit down and open my computer. It works, I have power. Skype pops open, and I call my house in Michigan without thinking about it. My mom's voice echoes across the line. "Hello?"

"Hey, it's Ellen."

"Ellie! How are you? We were praying for you every day."

"I . . ." My throat closes up, the tears are starting again, "Well . . ."

"Was it that bad?" She's all concern, this mother of mine.

"I, no, the tsunami zone was fine." I manage, and I'm a mess again. "But my friends are jerks!"

"Oh." She pauses. "Well . . . I wasn't really praying about that . . ."

38

Prayer Beads

Ellen

The funeral home looks like a community center designed by committee, set on an awkward one-way street behind a car dealership. The sign announces where we are in a no-nonsense Arial font. The automatic glass doors open with a whoosh, and I step into a sterile lobby. Workers wearing suits and white gloves greet and direct me to the desk where I can sign in.

I'm here to say good-bye to someone I never met and who didn't know me, but as my eyes meet those of Ito Sensei across the greeting desk, I feel a pang in my heart. He looks tired, which isn't unusual, and sad, which is an emotion I've never associated with him.

"Oh, Ellen Sensei, thank you so much for coming." He bows low, and I bow lower. We both rise and look at each other again. We're probably standing closer to each other than we ever do in class, but he seems much farther away today. "You've taken time out of your day to be here."

"It's not a problem." I reply. "I'm so sorry about your mother, I know she was sick."

"Yes, well." He bows again. "Thank you for coming."

"I don't have Buddhist prayer beads," I blurt out, groping into my purse and pulling out my rosary to show him. "So I brought my Christian ones, is that okay? I thought maybe I could pray . . ."

"Those will be perfect," he assures me, unfailingly kind. "My mother would be honored to have Christian prayers said for her as well."

"Okay." I bow once more and step aside to let the mourners behind me walk forward. Everyone is wearing black from head to toe, which extends, I realize, to their bags and accessories. I quickly wrap a black scarf around my traitorous orange purse. The devil is in the details.

Helpful attendants motion me into a large room off the lobby. The architecture makes it look like a convention center ballroom, but the decorations leave no doubt as to what this room is used for. Rows of precisely spaced black chairs face a wall that is decorated even more lavishly than the funeral store I once visited. Speaking of the funeral store—a familiar face turns toward me, and I find myself waved over to join Vice Principal Okamoto where he's sitting with Principal Ishiga.

"Ellen Sensei! I'm surprised to see you here." They move over a chair so I can sit at the end of the row. "How did you find it?"

"I Google-mapped the funeral home," I explain and stuff my inappropriately-colored bag under the chair where I can conceal it. "I didn't want to miss the wake."

"Of course not, you and Ito Sensei are very close, aren't you?" Principal Ishiga nods in approval. "You are a strong teaching team."

"Do you have any questions?" Mr. Okamoto asks, leaning forward. "She always has the most unexpected questions," he commiserates with Principal Ishiga.

"Oh . . . um . . ." I glance nervously around at the rapidly filling hall. "Do we have to do anything? Is there a ceremony? Or . . . speeches?"

"Nothing to worry about," he assures me. "Ito Sensei will speak for the family and then the priest will give a short sermon. Then we will all listen as he chants a sutra. Please pray along on your beads—you brought beads, right?" I show him my rosary, and he nods approvingly. "There may also be some incense we have to parcel out and burn, but you can just mimic what we do."

Relieved I won't be asked to prove my relation to the deceased or lead a prayer, I sit back and study the memorial at the front of the room. At the very center is a large framed portrait of Ito Sensei's mother. I've seen these kinds of pictures before, usually in the tatami rooms of my friends' homes. Her face is soft and gentle, and her smile is the same as her son's. Behind us, the priest enters, and we all stand to attention until he has taken his position with the family at the front of the room.

The ceremony proceeds as Mr. Okamoto said it would. I can't understand everything they say, but I don't need to. Instead, I reflect on Mrs. Ito and the wonderful son she raised. Whenever I encounter a kind person, I tend to give a lot of credit to his or her mother. To have produced a man as wonderful as Ito Sensei, his mother must have been quite a woman. I say a silent thank-you prayer to heaven, where I'm sure she is. Well, unless **Buddhism** has got the right of it, and in that case I hope she's reborn into a very wonderful human family.

When it comes time for us to burn incense, we file up the center aisle, similar to the communion procession. When reaching the front, each person grasps a small portion of incense and places it onto red-hot coals to release the pungent fumes. I wonder what mix this is?

The ceremony ends. Ito Sensei precedes us out of the room, supporting his elderly father on his arm. Ushers start at the rows closest to the door, so I settle back to wait for my turn to stand and leave. Other attendees peer at me curiously, no doubt wondering what I'm doing there. It doesn't bother me, I just concentrate on keeping my purse firmly wrapped in my scarf.

When my time comes to leave, I let Principal Ishiga and Vice Principal Okamoto go first. As we near the door I realize that everyone is stopping to say a few words to Ito Sensei and his father. Panic grips me—I forgot to ask what to say! As the line inches forward, I wrack my brains. Ito Sensei, I know, will be fine with my English profession of condolence, but what will I say to his father? A straight-up translation of "I'm sorry for your loss" will undoubtedly be wrong. All the variations I know for "sorry" won't work either. Why didn't I think to ask about this?

Mr. Okamoto moves aside, and now I'm face to face with Ito Sensei again. He looks more tired than before, but suddenly the smile I saw in his mother's portrait creases his features. "Ah, Ellen Sensei, many people are surprised to see an American girl here. Thank you very much for coming."

"No, not at all—." I start, but he interrupts me.

"May I introduce you to my father? He is very pleased to meet you. He was also an English teacher many years ago." He lays a hand on his father's shoulder where he sits in a low chair, and I lean down to make my introduction.

"It's very nice to make your acquaintance," I stutter. "I'm Ellen, I work with your son."

"You are the woman he teaches with?" Two dark brown eyes that show none of the frailty of his age lock with mine. "Atsushi, you've told me about her."

"Yes, Father, this is Ellen Sensei, who has helped me very much in class."

The older man reaches for my hand and grasps it. "Thank you for working with my son. I'm grateful that you've taken care of him."

I want to protest that nothing could be further from the truth. That, in fact, I wouldn't still be in Japan if not for Ito Sensei's mentorship. That he's taught me just as much as he's taught any of his thousands of students, but I can't. I have only enough time to bow to both of them again, accept a present of commemorative green tea, and leave the hall.

The wind catches my scarf as I step outside, uncovering my purse and revealing all my mistakes. Mr. Okamoto has waited for me by the entrance and smiles. "You did well, Ellen Sensei. I know Ito Sensei was very moved to see you."

"I don't feel like I did anything," I admit, looking down at the tea box in my hands. "I don't even know what to do with this tea."

"Just drink it," he advises me. "And as you do, remember Mrs. Ito. Remembering people," he reflects, "is important."

I couldn't agree more. The question is, how could I ever forget?

39

Caretakers of the Shrine

Jane

Dean is tired and hungry. Early in the morning, he drove to Ann Arbor from Kalamazoo, and then he rushed from meeting to meeting all day, missing both breakfast and lunch. He calls me as he pulls onto I-94 for the drive home, and I notice the slump in his voice. He agrees with my assessment and assures me that he will stop for something to eat, and that I shouldn't save any leftovers.

A half hour down the road, he is weighing the merits of Wendy's and Arby's when he spots the sign for exit 133, and his focus shifts.

Leaving the highway, he drives up the ramp, turns north, and after a couple of passes, locates what he thinks is the driveway that could lead to the statue of Mary in the bathtub. Three or four mailboxes and newspaper tubes mark the start of the long dirt two-track. A little way along are two orange signs: Private Drive and No Trespassing. There is an old metal gate that looks like it was left over from when this could have been a cow path, but the chain is down so Dean drives in. He rambles by the homes closest to the road, then a long marsh and a small pond ringed with cattails, eventually reaching a compound with a nondescript house and a large pole barn and garage. A pit bull mix rises and walks to the end of the chain on its house, remaining silent but staring. Dean parks at a respectful distance and walks to the front porch, rings the bell, and steps back to admire the three-foot-tall golden Buddha next to the front door.

Dean tries to ignore the low growl of the dog and rings the bell again. The door opens partway, and the gap is filled by a heavyset man wearing sandals, a pair of cut-off sweatpants, and no shirt. His torso is marked by the largest scar Dean has ever seen, a mottled reddish purple gash an inch or more wide and running from the base of his neck, over his navel to somewhere below his waistline. He holds a partially consumed hamburger in his right hand and the door in his left, and waits to see what the trespasser in a sport coat, tie, and leather shoes could possibly want badly enough to drive down the well-marked drive and past his guard dog.

Standing at the foot of the porch steps, Dean tells the story of two years of praying every time we drove to Detroit, and he asks if the Mary statue belongs to him. The man relaxes and steps out, saying a few quick words to his dog, who quiets and lies down. The owner softens his stare, and then smiles—and Dean notices that he resembles the Buddha figure. A little.

The Mary statue does belong to him, sort of.

The man moved into the house two years before. The previous owner let him know about the little highway shrine. That resident had not placed the Mary grotto up on the hill, and neither had the couple before him, who had owned the place for more than a decade. But like the owners who had gone before all of them, they had taken care to maintain the steep path, to mow the grass, and to keep the brush trimmed back so the statue would be visible from the highway one hundred feet below.

The man with the Buddha statue is not Catholic and has no idea if the previous residents were.

"The way I look at it, since the other owners had bothered to keep it up, I may as well, too. I'm glad it's important to someone."

Dean thanks the man for his tending and for his story. The man nods and smiles. They shake hands, and Dean climbs back in the car, turns around, and heads for home, his physical hunger forgotten.

After hearing Dean's story, here are the questions that grow day by day in my heart:

Does God prompt three people, over many years, to keep Mary standing above a busy highway so that some parents taking their daughter to the airport will remember to pause a moment and pray? Could God possibly be that foolish?

And does God love jizo shrines too? Does he send Christian daughters to Japan to tend a neglected jizo so that the suffering Japanese people will know how much they are loved?

Does God instruct us to remove our shoes on holy ground and then provide us with grass sandals to climb the mountain?

And does God prompt a Lutheran to go in search of the guardians of the Virgin Mary to tell one of them that his calling matters?

Can God possibly be this sweet?

40

Meaning of the Jizo

Ellen

Summer cross-country practice is in full swing this morning as I jog out to the grounds to watch the students—and to tend my jizo, of course. Tohaku Junior High is one of the top schools in running, having dominated Central Tottori cross-country for the past three years. We advanced as far as the national competition, and both boy and girl runners participated in the Junior Olympics held in Tokyo. The cross-country coaches demand complete commitment.

This year is the same, with students running more than three kilometers every morning as the temperature climbs into the 90s. Students initially train in their club teams until they can be sorted into speed/distance classes. Once the coaches have determined the top performers, detailed training schedules are drawn up for a three-month period leading up to the regional qualifiers.

It's not just a school tradition. Whole families run together here in Kotoura, including several citywide cross-country events and a local marathon in which thousands participate. Good runners are respected and well-known, not only in the school halls, but in the local community. Even I have grudgingly taken up running since coming here. Not to do so would make me something of a pariah.

Though I will occasionally run with the students in the morning, I am not as diligent about my exercise as I am about continuing to ask the jizo to keep these kids safe. He's done a good job, no major mishaps or accidents, and all the students are energetic enough to finish their four-hour club practices in the afternoon, even after the three- kilometer run every morning.

I'm returning from the spigot with a full cup of water when I meet the substitute gym teacher. A slim, cultured man with something of a movie-star quality about him, he's standing in for one of our tenured teachers who is recovering from surgery. From the two months we've worked together, I know that his day job isn't teaching. He serves as a priest at a large temple in nearby Kurayoshi. Priests officiate blessings, funerals, and various other ceremonies, similar to the Christian variety. In their free time, they are also allowed to pursue other fields, in his case, teaching physical education.

He spots the cup in my hand. "Ellen Sensei, where did you get that?"

I motion for him to come with me, and I explain on the way. "A while ago I found a jizo statue back here by the pool." He's looking at me curiously, and I quickly add, "Everyone had forgotten about it, so I take care of it. I give it water and flowers sometimes."

He's still staring at me, and I blush a bit. Maybe as a Buddhist priest he's offended that a non-Buddhist is taking care of the shrine. I never thought about it, but if I found a Buddhist person taking care of a bathtub Mary I might be a bit affronted. My explanation falters as we reach the jizo. "Jizos protect children, you see . . . so I just wanted him to be clean and happy so he'd protect the students well."

I stop. It's kind of silly to explain a religion to its own priest. Not sure what to do, I settle with placing the cup carefully in its usual spot and brushing a bit of dirt off the placement stone.

He kneels down next to me and observes the jizo for a moment. "You know a lot about Japanese religion, Ellen Sensei."

"Not as much as you," I object. "But I studied jizos in college, and I knew what it was when I found this one."

"Jizos don't just protect living children," he tells me, rearranging some of the coins piled on the ground. "Specifically, jizos care for children who die before their parents."

"Oh." I didn't know that. "How do they protect them?"

"If children die young, they haven't had time to do enough good things to carry them across the river to the afterlife," he explains, turning the cup slightly. "So Ojizo-sama hides them under his cloak from the demons and sings them the mantras."

This is new to me. So Ojizo-sama is helping those souls stuck in a sort of Buddhist purgatory? How interesting. I hadn't realized that.

"Do you know why this jizo is here?" he asks. "It's been here for almost thirty years, now."

"Thirty years?" *That's not so long. I had thought it was older.* I'm about to ask more, but he's continuing anyway.

"I used to be a student here at Tohaku Junior High," he tells me. "And thirty years ago there was an accident."

This is new. "What happened?"

"It was a friend of mine. We'd been in the same class since grade school. He joined the cross-country team that summer and was practicing on a hot day. A lot like today, actually."

Despite the rising morning temperature, I'm getting chills. "Did he get hurt?"

"He died." The gym teacher's gaze is fixed on the statue. "Ran too hard. His parents erected this jizo in his honor."

We're silent. I can hear the runners circling the track behind me, and my heart breaks thinking of such a thing happening to any of them. I'm suddenly, fervently, so grateful that I've been tending this statue, even if I didn't know exactly why. I send up a spontaneous prayer. Not only for my current students, but for the poor boy whose death years ago prompted this statue's presence.

"Thank you for tending this jizo." We get back to our feet, and he bows formally to me. "I think his parents would be very happy to know you are caring for it."

"Oh, it's nothing," I reply in my best formal Japanese, since the situation seems to call for it.

Hearing my polite phrasing, he laughs and smiles warmly at me. "It seems, Ellen Sensei, that you have a Japanese soul."

He walks back to the practice and I ponder his words. I'm not sure if my soul is Japanese, or American, or something else entirely, but I'm growing increasingly certain that, no matter what kind of soul it is, it's loved. And whether I'm doing good deeds to get across a river or through a set of pearly gates, ultimately, love will steer me true.

Glossary

ALT
Assistant Language Teacher

Buddhism
Buddhism was founded in India in the fifth century B.C. The tradition traces its origin to Siddhartha Gautama, who is typically referred to as the Buddha. Two-thirds of the Japanese population is affiliated with Buddhism in some way.

catechesis
the process of teaching religion in the Catholic Church

Ellen-kai
Ellen-meeting

Ganbatte
Do your best.

JET
Japanese Exchange and Teaching Program

Miraculous Medal
St. Catherine Laboure, a young nun in the first part of the nineteenth century in Paris, France, was given the design for this medal in a vision

of the Virgin Mary. Its wide and rapid distribution and reputation for miracles led it to being called "miraculous" by the faithful.

Naruto
a popular Japanese animated television program and comic about ninjas

O.G.A. for Aid
a volunteer organization started by the Ortiz family in the aftermath of the tsunami disaster

Ojizo-sama/jizo
Jizo is the Japanese name of one of the most popular bodhisattvas in Japan and is usually used in conjunction with the honorifics *O* and *sama*. *Jizo* statues are a familiar sight along roadsides in Japan.

quilted heating table
a table with heating coils on the underside and a quilted skirt that traps the heat underneath, forming a sort of tent

sakura
the flowering cherry trees in Japan

Sensei
teacher

Shintoism
Shinto, the native religion of Japan, is the largest religion in the country, practiced by nearly 80 percent of the population. There are 100,000 Shinto shrines and 20,000 priests.

Society of St. Vincent de Paul
a Catholic lay organization founded in 1833 by college students in Paris, France. The Society helps 14 million poor people around the world

Sumimasen

I'm sorry; pardon me; excuse me.

tatami

woven straw mats used as flooring in many Japanese buildings

the Island of Knights and Knaves

a fictional place invented by mathematician Raymond Smullyon in his book, *What Is the Name of This Book?* Smullyon creates logic puzzles with the characters as an exercise in mathematical reasoning.

Acknowledgments

I am grateful to everyone who helped us write this book and nurse it through to publication. To Dean and Martha, who read the first drafts and helped with my recollections. My writer's group: Katie, Bess, Gretchen, Sheila, Jim, Joyce, and Ginny are wonderful writers themselves, and they are also wonderful parents. Our conversations about placing our trembling faith into the hands of the next generation were the headwaters of the stream that became *Love Will Steer Me True*. They disagreed, questioned, advised, and always encouraged me. I'm glad I threw that first chapter away.

My geometry students at St. Monica School in Kalamazoo gave me one of the best years of my teaching career. They also gave me some good stories. Thank you for allowing me to share your eighth-grade year with readers.

To Father Tom, who told me how healing works. I've been listening better ever since.

The staff at Loyola Press trusted us to come through with a book after reading five sample chapters. Those people have courage. Thank you to Joe, Vinita, Rosemary, Beth, Steve, Andrew, and Becca for your enthusiastic support.

Faith is a gift from God. But I only recognized the gift because I knew some other people who already had it: my parents, Pat and

Dottie Hudson; my in-laws, Max and Lorraine Knuth; and my husband, Dean. I am so very grateful that you passed on what God gave you, even when I didn't seem to appreciate it at the time.

Jane

I'd like, first and foremost, to thank my mom, who was the driving force behind transforming me from an accidental author to a published writer. There is truly no better motivation to finish a manuscript than being locked in a hotel room with your coauthor.

Thank you to my sister, dad, students, coworkers, and friends who so graciously allowed me to write about them!

I am humbled and amazed by O.G.A. for Aid and their continued work in the Tohoku region. There is much left to be done! If you wish to volunteer or donate, please visit their website: www.ogaforaid.org/en/

Thank you to the family and friends of Rodger Swan, a man who touched so many people with his positivity and kindness. Western Michigan University maintains a memorial scholarship in his honor; please consider donating: www.wmich.edu/languages/rodgerswan

To my two pre-readers, Holly Long and Michael Joseph Radke, more thanks than words can express. Your feedback and comments were hugely encouraging and helped me stay true.

The wonderful editors and staff at Loyola Press are the best any author could ever hope for. I still can't believe my luck!

Finally, Kotoura and Tohaku Junior High School. This book may be the longest thank-you letter ever written, but the length is justified.

Ellen

About the Authors

Jane Knuth has been volunteering at the St. Vincent de Paul thrift store in Kalamazoo, Michigan, for the past nineteen years. A part-time math tutor, Jane also teaches Ukrainian Easter egg decorating, does hand bookbinding, and writes a monthly column for *The Good News*, the newspaper of the Diocese of Kalamazoo. She and her husband, Dean, live in Portage, Michigan, and have two daughters, Ellen and Martha.

In 2011, Jane's first book, *Thrift Store Saints*, was awarded first place from the Catholic Press Association for Popular Presentation of the Catholic Faith.

Ellen Knuth recently returned to the USA after five years in Japan. Having already been an English teacher, a singer in a rock band, a dairy princess, an MC, and a newspaper columnist, Ellen now works as a university relations manager for a study- and intern-abroad company. Settled (for now) in Clinton Township, Michigan, she travels extensively, writes occasionally, and sings constantly.

This is Ellen's first book.